Gone Bush

Spence Burn Biv, Takitimu Mountains, Southland, 2002.

Gone Bush

A LIFE IN THE BACKCOUNTRY AND BEYOND

Paul Kilgour

HarperCollins*Publishers*

HarperCollins*Publishers*
Australia • Brazil • Canada • France • Germany • Holland • Hungary
India • Italy • Japan • Mexico • New Zealand • Poland • Spain • Sweden
Switzerland • United Kingdom • United States of America

First published in 2021
by HarperCollins*Publishers* (New Zealand) Limited
Unit D1, 63 Apollo Drive, Rosedale, Auckland 0632, New Zealand
harpercollins.co.nz

A catalogue record for this book is available from the National Library of New Zealand

ISBN 978 1 7755 4173 8 (pbk)
ISBN 978 1 7754 9204 7 (ebook)

Cover design by Mietta Yans, HarperCollins Design Studio
Front cover image: Brewster Hut, Mt Aspiring National Park by Bec Kilpatrick/Getty Images
Back cover image: Slaty Creek Hut, Westland, 1977
Unless otherwise credited, all photos are taken by or are from the collection of Paul Kilgour
Typeset in Adobe Garamond Pro by Kirby Jones

To all who wander

Preface

I remember a trip in steep country in the Pyke Valley, Fiordland National Park. There were four of us moving through the bush on an unmarked trail about 50 metres above Lake Wilmot. My three companions all stepped across a small stream. As I went to follow, I sensed something moving above, and glanced upstream. A rock about the size of a caravan was rolling towards us. I scrambled back, the other three sprinted forward, and the rock went crashing past and on down the stream. As it gathered speed it wound up every strand of bush lawyer and supplejack from the surrounding bush, until the combined strength almost brought it to a halt. Suddenly everything snapped, vines whipping like high-tension wires, and the rock took off again, smashing through the bush and plunging into the lake. At that point every bird in the valley went ballistic.

Welcome to the serene pastime that is tramping in New Zealand.

Recently, I clocked up 50 years of it. I was a sheltered 20-year-old from a North Auckland farm when I ventured, dazzled, into the epic South Island backcountry on my first tramping trip. The following weekend, I bagged my first hut, a cosy four-bunker on a tributary of the Waimakariri River in Arthur's Pass National Park. There was a heavy frost underfoot the next morning, but the sun soon cleared the top of the beech forest to warm us as we prepared to leave. Watching my companions re-lay the fire for the next group of trampers, I felt like an initiate to some long-established guild – although, in fact, recreational tramping was only a generation or two deep in those first years of the 1970s, and still fringe. When I started, it was possible to walk through somewhere like the Abel Tasman National Park and see virtually nobody – a terrific time to get bitten by the tramping bug.

And get bitten I did. In late 2019, on the Round the Mountain Track at Ruapehu, I bagged my 1200th hut. Last month, I knocked off my 1208th, a 'secret' (okay, illegal) hunters' hut in the hills beyond Tākaka. They've come in all shapes and sizes, from ramshackle two-man bivvies to the new generation of Department of Conservation (DOC) mega-huts, and from Northland to the Subantarctic Islands. I don't dwell on the tally so much as what those 1200-odd huts represent – a lifetime of wandering that began long before I even knew what 'tramping' was, when I was a five-year-old disappearing into the scrub beyond our Waimauku farm. It reached its zenith in 2008 when I walked the length of the South Island, from deepest Fiordland to my home in Golden Bay.

It's a life peopled with backcountry characters who you don't often see now, the type who, like me, were happiest on the hoof or holed up in a remote bivvy: swaggers, recluses, latter-day prospectors and high-country musterers. It's a life enlarged by an intimate association with our glorious outdoors, from the alps to the coast and all parts between, but always and especially the New Zealand bush.

For me, the bush is the place where nothing else seems to matter, and being there is everything. The air is clear; the world is quiet; time stops. My ideal, which I've experienced on longer walks, is to reach a point where you have no idea what day of the week it is. On a few trips, I haven't taken a watch. I found I slept when I needed to, started walking when I felt like it, ate when I was hungry. I was tuning in to natural rhythms, into the bush, the mountains, and to myself. You feel part of nature, no more special than the birds in the trees or any other creature. I've had my battles with depression, and in those times the bush is often a solace.

Max Polglaze is a former Forest Service ranger, and an old friend. Before I met him, however, I knew him from his bush poetry, scribbled in hut books in his Mt Arthur-Leslie-Kahurangi bailiwick. I copied one out once because it summed up my feeling about the bush:

> My heart is in the valley of a thousand memories,
> of campfire nights and sundrenched days and tall majestic trees.
> Of sparkling crystal waters and the birdsong on the rise,
> in the fair and lovely country of this bushland paradise.

More practically, I've maintained a lifelong habit of keeping logbooks. Half a century on, there are half a dozen of them stashed in a shed at our house at Rangihaeata. The early ones are very matter-of-fact. Of my first tramp, all that's noted is '15 July, 1972, Richardson Track'. But they soon grow more descriptive and engaging. I'm constantly 'zooming' up valleys or 'charging' across rivers, and I begin to name my tramping companions, if there happen to be any. Reading these later journals transports me straight into the deep bush and tussocklands of those adventures, and they've proved a handy route guide for the account that follows. Most of it takes place in the South Island backcountry, but it begins, as my wanderings did, in a sleepy settlement north of Auckland.

Lonely Lake Hut, Kahurangi National Park, 2015.

Chapter 1

I was born in Helensville in 1951 and grew up on the family farm near Waimauku, a small farming community inland north-east of Muriwai Beach. From a very young age, I had a fair bit of freedom and plenty of territory to explore.

The farm was on Highway 16, the main road north of Auckland to Helensville. It was a gravel road back then, seven cars a week if we were lucky. If you saw a green van coming, well then it must be 2 pm on a Thursday, because that's when Mrs Gardener does her shopping. Life was so predictable. The telephone operator would phone and say, 'Does anyone know anyone with a black Wolseley? There's a black Wolseley coming up the road!' Heavens, a stranger! That same road now has tens of thousands of car movements a day.

My father Bob Kilgour was born on Jersey Island, and had his fourth birthday as his family sailed out to this part of the world, a one-way trip to the colonies. His mother Ivy was from several generations of French-speaking Jersey Islanders, and his father Douglas was a Scotsman – and, according to family legend, his father, Robert, was the illegitimate child of King Edward. They stepped off the boat at Onehunga Harbour, walked up the road, saw a little house with a pōhutukawa tree out front, and thought, 'This'll do.' Eventually my grandparents got work as milkers on a dairy farm near Kumeu, and after a few years, they bought the farm at Waimauku.

Mum was Dorna deRaine Brasington. The middle name was a tip of the hat to her maternal French grandfather, Jules deRaine, around whom an air of intrigue and possible scandal floated. I never met him, but growing up I gained the impression that there was some perceived disgrace about Jules that made adults clam up. Recently, a relative of mine reported that his grave had been found in an overgrown corner of a Māori cemetery in Dargaville, with a headstone inscribed in both French and te reo Māori. It's a mystery I'd dearly love to solve, but I fear the answer may have died with my mother.

Mum's dad was the wonderfully named Silas Augustus Phillip Brasington. As a kid, what struck me most about my grandfather Silas was his sense of theatre. When he wrote out cheques, for instance, he would sign every one of his names. It practically covered the entire cheque, but always with beautiful penmanship. I remember watching him sign one at Wrightson's, and slowly people started coming over to witness this work of art unfold. He stopped, looked up at the assistant, and said, 'Just one more moment, lad,' then carried on dotting all the Is and crossing the Ts before handing it over with the comment, 'My mother always told me I should have been an artist.'

He had emigrated from Australia as a 20-year-old with a grand total of 20 shillings in his pocket. He laboured on farms, became a buttermaker and then according to family history played a significant role in establishing New Zealand's early cooperative dairy system – although I've never found anything official giving him credit. The story I heard was that he got a position managing a New Zealand Dairy Company factory in Mt Eden – I know, Mt Eden sounds an odd location for a dairy factory, but that's what I was told – and then moved the family to Waimauku to establish a cooperative factory there.

My parents met on Mum's first morning at Waimauku primary school. She took the only spare seat left, next to Bob Kilgour, who at eight was her senior by a year. A friendship blossomed, and later a romance.

When Mum was 13, Silas was offered the position of managing a butter factory in London and the family decamped from Waimauku. They weren't there long before war broke out. My grandfather felt obliged to keep the factory on track – butter was now classed an essential item – but Mum was given a choice: return to New Zealand, or stay with her family. She chose to stay, and suffered through the Blitz. She saw some horrible things and was permanently scarred by the experience. Years later, she would cringe whenever an airplane went overhead.

Back in Waimauku, Dad's father Douglas had been struggling with the effects of a terrible accident. He'd seen some men struggling to hand-crank a vehicle on the local air-force base and when he went to help, the crank handle had rocketed into his head. He eventually died of complications arising from the injury and at the tender age of 16, Dad had to take over running the farm.

All this time, he and Mum had been writing to each other. There's a strange story about their communication. Dad was a ham radio enthusiast. One night on his homemade crystal radio set he heard an SOS from a British flying boat, the *Calpurnia*, which flew mail between Australia and Britain during the war. It crashed and the radio operator, the only survivor, sent out an SOS but then died. Months later, some mail that Mum had sent to Dad was returned to her, marked as having been recovered in a damaged state from the wreckage of the *Calpurnia*. The aircraft whose SOS Dad heard had been carrying a love letter from Mum.

Even though communication was more complicated back then, it seemed easier to keep a relationship alive. And the horrors of the war would have added another element, that deep yearning for someone special on the other side of the world. When Mum got back to New Zealand, she and Dad picked up where they left off. They soon became pregnant (this was before they married, which must have been a bit scandalous), but sadly suffered a miscarriage.

Perhaps that was why Mum's parents seemed to suddenly develop a dislike of Dad. My maternal grandmother was a terrible snob – I've only ever seen one photo of her with the hint of a smile; in all the rest she's stony-faced – so maybe it was a class thing. In any case, they told Dad that if he wanted to marry their daughter he'd have to stump up an acre of land on the Kilgour farm for them to live on. (Dad's mum lived close by us, too. With hindsight I know I probably should have spent more time learning from those old people.)

My parents married in 1950 and I was born soon after, followed by Barry, then Ross. My brothers and I are chalk and cheese. I was the black sheep of the family, the weakling, a scrawny thing, the one who got into mischief – or was blamed for it. They are both much more typical farmer's sons, right down to their stockier build.

It was a small farm – but then they all were compared with today's corporate operations. We started with 28 cows and that was considered a viable farming proposition. When it grew to 45 animals, it was one of the largest herds in the district. People would say, 'Forty-five cows! Hope they know what they're doing.' Today's 1000-strong herds would have been inconceivable back then, when having 100-odd productive cows was considered good enough to justify establishing a butter factory.

Nevertheless, my parents struggled financially. Once, they even seriously contemplated selling the farm. I remember breaking open my savings, holding out a few paltry shillings and asking, 'Would this help?' (I got told off for smashing a perfectly good piggybank.) But perhaps the money worries led to Dad looking for other work, because when I was about five he was offered a job as caretaker/park ranger on Kāpiti Island. I remember feeling so happy – that fascination I have with wild places was clearly already there, and what five-year-old boy wouldn't be excited by the idea of living on a remote conservation island? Sadly for me, Mum didn't want to leave her parents, so it didn't happen.

As a member of the local cooperative dairy factory, Dad was rostered to work half a day every month at the Waimauku butter factory, and I would usually tag along. The co-op had a truck that could be used to collect the cans of milk and cream from beside the various farm gates, but most of the farmers used their own vehicle. In our case, Dad had an old Indian motorbike with a sidecar and I'd sit in that, trundling down the highway, stacking up cans on the sidecar's foot platform as we went.

The factory was a typical pre-war concrete and tin thing. These days it's a restaurant and craft store, and you'll often see that with ex-dairy factories – they built those things to last! Inside it was dominated by big, squat stainless-steel cream vats, about the height of a man but much broader, with ladders set alongside. My job was to climb to the top of the vats and use a net to haul out any dead rats. We'd throw them out the back door to where all the stray dogs congregated. What a treat for a dog – freshly creamed rat! As for us humans, the butter from the Waimauku factory was always a hundred times yellower, richer and more delicious than anything store-bought, and that went for anything home-raised, home-baked or homemade in our eyes.

At the age of five, I began to disappear from home at night. I'd wake up in darkness with no inkling of the time but ready for an adventure, so I'd climb out the window and be gone. Often it was moonlight that drew me, and the stillness. As a kid of the 1950s, your days were driven by an expectation that you would be a nice and polite child. At night, when everyone else was asleep, I felt I had the freedom to follow my true nature.

I'd walk the farm until I collapsed. Dad would find me in the barn where the dogs and orphaned farm animals slept, curled up among hay bales, surrounded by calves and piglets. Sometimes he'd come across me in a paddock sleeping beside a cow for warmth. It was the beginning of a lifetime of wandering. I wasn't going to be a North Auckland farmer – or indeed anything that required me to be tethered to one place for long.

Our property was 120 acres. There was an 1100-acre sheep farm across the road, and another farm up the back, and lots of bushy gullies that no one seemed to own, along with marae land nearby. All of it connected to sand dune country that led to Muriwai Beach. After a while, I began to range beyond our farm and to journey during daylight hours, walking what were really vast distances for a little fella. It wasn't called 'tramping', and I didn't think of it that way. It was just me running away from school or home, or heading out to the coast to collect some shellfish. A lot of this adventuring was unknown to my parents or teachers. As my brothers got older they'd occasionally tag along, but mostly I was alone – and happily so. I never felt in the least bit lonely or nervous, but rather that there was a big wide world out there waiting for me.

I did it all barefoot; that was how all of us district kids got around. In school photos from that era, almost no one is wearing shoes. If someone ever turned up wearing socks and shoes, even if it was winter, they'd get a puzzled look from the rest of us, and next day they'd be barefoot again. If the morning was especially cold and frosty, we'd warm our frozen feet in a nicely steaming cow pat. Our townie friends found it disgusting, but we thought it was a perfectly sensible solution.

Like my parents, I attended Waimauku School. I had learning challenges from the start – dyslexia, although it wasn't diagnosed as such. When we had to write things from the blackboard I'd get down each letter one at a time, but then I'd struggle to put the words together. Every week we'd be asked to choose a book to read and write about. How on earth could I do that? In those days, they just stuck you in what was colloquially called the 'dummy class' and left you to it. I was puzzled – I know I'm a bit different, but why I am here? – and I also felt hurt. It certainly aggravated my rebellious streak.

When my primary school was organising its 100th anniversary (for 2021), they asked if I'd talk about life in the 1950s. I warned them it wouldn't all be particularly positive. This was an era when they were trying to beat the Māori language out of everyone. A lot of my friends at school were Māori and we'd often use Māori words, just really basic terms sprinkled in with our English, such as 'kia ora e hoa', 'ka pai' and 'mōrena'. We often defaulted to Māori names (I was 'Paora'), and if something was broken or stuffed it was always 'pakaru'. We were strapped for it, and I developed very strong calluses on my hands.

I was strapped, too, for using my left hand. (As an adult, I use both, and really the only thing I can't do with my left hand is write well.) The more they punished me, the more I felt for others who are ostracised for being different. For example, I had a friend who was a bad stutterer. A new teacher once yelled at him, 'Don't you dare stutter at me, boy!' When I explained that he couldn't help it, she started yelling at me, and we were both marched off to the headmaster and punished for being cheeky. I learned a lot about discrimination as a result of those incidents, and became stronger in my convictions.

I had a sensitivity that was a little different, as well as a willingness to speak out. We used to have compulsory religious study once a week. The guy was a racist and had a horrible attitude. I used to challenge him on things and he would scream at me. I thought, 'I'm getting out of here.' During religious instruction, the Catholics were all required to sit out in a little shelter shed on the edge of the school grounds, so I decided I was going to be a Catholic. Then I discovered the shed was right next to the surrounding trees, and that I could disappear into the bush. So of course, I did exactly that.

In 'dummy class' I had more opportunities to vanish. In those days, there wasn't much of a curriculum for 'special students', and we were given plenty of free time in the playground, which included an area of scrub and pine trees. There was a bit of a creek near the school, swampy in places, and a rough tangle of blackberry bordering one of the mowed edges of the school grounds. One day, I got on my stomach and crawled under the blackberry and through to the other side.

I can still remember how it felt. It was a sense of escape, mixed with a feeling of arriving in exactly the right place.

It's hard to pin down, but I experience the same thing now when I'm tramping somewhere that I've never been before. It was also about realising how magic your legs are – that they can take you anywhere.

Beyond the blackberry you were into a different world of bracken, scrub and mānuka – which to a kid looked like forest. After that came large pines, some tōtara and rimu, then a fence, scrubby farmland, and finally mature kauri forest. It was amazing to be among such huge and ancient trees. And the birdlife! I loved birds; I think that's why I developed such a fascination with aviation. Sometimes, when I heard an aircraft passing overhead, I'd run out of the classroom for a look, the teacher bellowing at me, 'Come back this instant!' To this day I still drop whatever I'm doing and run outside to watch an aircraft fly overhead.

Once in the bush, I kept going. I didn't have a watch, but I was tuned in to time, and knew when I had to turn back. I was never declared missing, so nobody found out. I'd meet a farmer or two – these were the days when farmers walked everywhere or went on horse – but no one ever asked me why I wasn't in school. It wasn't an issue. I'd return with massive scratches all over my legs, prickles in my feet, and bee stings from running barefoot through fields.

Likewise, my parents didn't have a clue just how far off-track I could go while apparently walking home from school. They imagined that I strolled up the railway lines, through the neighbours' farm to home. In fact, I'd sneak off to the railway station, where I'd become friendly with the station master. A big Māori fella, he'd say, 'Boy, you're in luck today, Uncle is coming up the line and he'll give you a ride.' He was talking about a particular engineer on the daily freight train from Auckland to Ōpua in the Bay of Islands. The train wasn't scheduled to stop at our station, but the engineer would bring this great fire-breathing dragon to a screeching halt, and yell, 'Hop on, boy!' I'd climb up, a barefoot kid hopping to avoid hot embers, shovelling coal into the firebox as we went steaming up the tracks.

Every time I'd go just a little bit further, because I wanted to walk back through new country. I'd have to run home to make up time. I don't know how many miles I ran home! I was seven, eight years old. They were different times, and I'm so pleased to have known them.

There were people living in little huts all over the place, usually elderly Māori – there was a lot of Māori land around those parts. I recall one old couple who lived in a hut in the scrub at the end of a long walk up a bush track. Today it's what you'd call 'living off the grid', but it's just what people did back then. Boy, were they welcoming, always offering me a homemade fruit juice and chatting away, often in Māori. I learned a lot of new words and expressions from them.

Their whare intrigued me – in fact, it's probably where my fascination with huts began. It was a very basic shelter, with a roof of rusty iron that was constantly being patched with more pieces of rusty iron, and walls of rough-sawn timber. They had an earth floor that was almost shiny from being constantly swept using a broom made of ferns tied to a stick. Another hut I saw on my travels had what was either rimu or tōtara poles as framing, and was clad in vertical sheets of iron, with a big porch and long overhangs to keep it dry and a tank to collect rainwater.

As you got nearer the coast and Muriwai Beach you came across baches. These were very basic structures that some people lived in year-round. None of them was ever locked – I didn't see my first lock until after I'd left school. There used to be an understanding about baches, that you could stop and take shelter. These days it's all holiday homes that are like mansions and are only used for a few weeks of the year – what a waste!

When I was about six or seven I went on a mission to Muriwai to collect toheroa – we were allowed 20 per person a day, which was a heavy sackload for a little kid like me – and got caught out in a big storm. I could hear rain pelting down on a tin roof somewhere; what a welcome sound that was – and still is! I found a cute little one-room bach and stayed there until the rain eased. I ate some baked beans I found on a shelf and left a note to say thanks. My parents roughly knew where I was and probably assumed I'd find shelter. Certainly they trusted all of us kids to be able to look after ourselves out there. In retrospect, that independence and freedom was a wonderful gift.

I've since tried to retrace my old wandering routes around Waimauku, but there are now so many blocks of land with 'Private Property, Keep Out' signs that it's impossible. It's a totally different world, almost unrecognisable, and people now take a far less generous view of strangers walking over their land.

It was a time in New Zealand when no one had much money – even on our farm we didn't seem to have anything to spend – but everyone helped others. If a cow got stuck in a ditch, the neighbours would bowl up and collectively we'd haul it out – and the same went for trucks and cars that went off the road or broke down. As dairy farmers, we shared the milk, and that generosity was returned in kind. We were given fruit and veges that we couldn't grow ourselves, and in the autumn locals dropped off loads of firewood. I also remember a time when our pump shed broke down and our neighbours trucked in water to fill our troughs. If there were roadworks nearby, Mum would always wander down with a plate of warm date scones for the road workers, and invariably we'd find a load of gravel beside our drive the next day. As a result of those experiences, I've always been a strong believer in what goes around comes around.

Another strong influence growing up was that we lived in a largely Māori community. Most of my friends at primary and high school were Māori kids – Adrian Akarana, Valerie Fenton – the Fentons were a big local Māori family – and the Temu kids. Reweti marae was just up the road and during my wanderings I'd often call in for a drink of water and some food from the aunties.

In 1963, the marae was at the centre of an awful tragedy, the so-called Brynderwyn Bus Disaster, which is still New Zealand's worst road accident. That 7 February, the Queen and the Duke of Edinburgh were at Waitangi, and a bus chartered by the Māori Affairs Department took 35 people from the district up there to be part of it. Coming back over the Brynderwyn Hills the next day, the bus's brakes failed and it plunged from a 30-metre cliff into a gully. Fifteen died, including a number of older people from Reweti marae. Usually when something awful like that happens it's the elders who look after the younger ones and keep everything together. This time, the traditional comforters were gone.

*

In my last couple of years at school we got a new teacher, Miss Chapple, who turned out to be pretty radical. She'd play folk music to us, the likes of Joan Baez and Bob Dylan, and talk about the meaning of their songs, and what these Vietnam protests were really all about. To me, it all made total sense. She had twin babies that she'd breastfeed during class. To us farm kids that was also perfectly natural.

She emphasised that 'special classes' were called 'special' for good reason, and that we kids had unique characteristics. God, I admire her for saying that. It was a turning point for me. I used to think, 'Why am I this scrawny, different kid? Why can't I be someone else, someone sporty and brainy?' Now I started to feel strong about who I was. Sure I was different, but that was totally okay. Something clicked then about the exploring, too – this is what I do, and it's wonderful.

Mid-flat Hut, Hunter River Valley.

Chapter 2

I was four or five when I first met the swaggers. My brothers, who are two and six years younger than me, can't remember them at all, so it was a short-lived thing, very possibly the end of an era.

I had no concept of them being down-and-out or homeless. They were people who carried their homes on their backs. In my memory, they weren't lugging the traditional swag but instead had backpacks, possibly one of the early framed versions or a homemade equivalent with wooden frames. I definitely remember one of them carving some sort of decoration into his pack frame. In any case, I was totally beguiled: you could carry everything you needed in life on your back!

The other thing that intrigued me was how they used stones as a messaging system. A stone left on a fencepost, for example, might mean 'I was here'. A bush telegraph thing.

They'd turn up at our farm at milking time, help in the shed, feed the pigs and split wood. My dad was very welcoming. Mum was a bit more standoffish – 'Watch those people!' But whenever they were offered a bed in the house they always refused. They were at one with the outdoors; they didn't have any use for four walls and clean sheets.

The farm had big 100-year-old macrocarpas, and they often camped underneath, 400 metres or so from our house.

They used bricks for a fireplace. Dad would tell them to be careful with fire under the trees, and they always were. There was a stream nearby for their water, and Dad supplied them with a bucket.

They invariably had blocks of dripping for frying up their bread, and Dad would give them a bit of mutton to go with it. There was never anything green to be seen – although they probably feasted on potatoes, kūmara and shellfish when they found them. They used nooses to catch possums and rabbits, which they cooked over the fire. I can still almost smell that aroma of roasting rabbit! Some nights there'd be four or five swaggers around the campfire, telling stories and poems, describing their travels.

The swaggers had their particular 'rounds'. There was one swaggie whose round involved walking down the coast and living on seafood collected along the way. Others had places around Northland where they targeted being at a certain date. They'd put in crops – kūmara and spuds were popular – and return in time for the harvest. They were passing through what was private property, but no one worried. When they left the beach they'd have a sack of shellfish – toheroa, usually – and when they met locals they'd give them a few.

For one swagger, Waimauku was the southern end of his round. He'd go across to the east coast and work his way up as far as Russell, then go through to the Waipoua Forest and down the west coast. I don't know how he crossed the Kaipara – perhaps he got paddled across, because it's a huge harbour. Another guy was more dedicated to exploring inland Northland. A third sometimes went up to Kaitāia and Ninety Mile Beach, but he said that was really someone else's patch and he didn't venture too far. They weren't possessive, but they respected each other's patches. Another swagger used to travel to the outskirts of Auckland city itself. He'd head into the Waitākere Ranges or along the Manukau Harbour, or visit Riverhead and Devonport. They were little coastal villages back then, still with something of a sense of remoteness about them.

Some of these swaggers travelled with lightweight calico tents, others slept under trees or in hay barns. If it was raining and they couldn't find shelter, they'd keep walking. They wore homemade oilskin ponchos, which were really just ordinary sheets coated in horrible smelly stuff. One guy made tent cords out of harakeke. There certainly wasn't any foam or Therm-a-Rest to sleep on, but there was always something soft that could be found under the trees to use for bedding.

They worked at properties along the way, picking fruit, chopping wood, shearing. There never seemed to be any money involved; they'd work for a place to sleep and food. I found that fascinating, too, and it perhaps explains how I developed my anti-materialistic, socialist leanings. You work together, and everyone's happy.

When I was young, everyone in the countryside worked hard and walked everywhere and there wasn't a lot of obesity. I remember seeing my first overweight person at the age of ten. But these guys were particularly lean. When there was no food to be had, they just kept walking. I have a similar approach myself on my longer tramping trips: the more walking I do, the less I seem to need to eat to get charged up.

There might have been shame in some of their backgrounds. I remember an uncle saying, 'Oh, watch out for them, they're Remittance Men!' It made no sense at the time, but now I think he meant they'd been banished from Britain as a result of some disgrace, and money was sent to them to encourage them to not come back. Rumour had it that one of them might have been the illegitimate child of royalty. Who knows? It was certainly a hard life for some of them. I read a sad story once about a farmer who found a swagger frozen to death beside the road. No one knew who he was, so he was buried nearby in an anonymous grave.

I didn't feel any fear of the swaggers. I still try to give people the benefit of the doubt – see the positive and work on that. To me they were amazing, and as a result I had some wonderful talks with them. I was on their list of people to meet along the way. They'd say, 'Ah, I've heard about you, young fella.'

I'd sneak out of my room at night and head up to their camp under the trees to listen to their stories. I don't know what they were drinking – I thought it was tea – but I remember a lot of raucousness and jolly laughter, poetry and singing, and no sense at all of down-and-out-ness. Whether they had a feeling of freedom, or were just content with what little they had, I don't know. Now people are very aware of what they haven't got, but there was a different vibe then. Mind you, I was a kid at the time, so there was probably a lot I missed.

I remember names – although it's possible I muddle some of them with the swaggers that they yarned about. One guy was known as The Shiner. Later I found out that he'd spent time in Golden Bay and Nelson, and travelled the Heaphy Track as part of his round – hence the name of a stream on the track called Shiner Brook. I'm not sure if he's the Shiner of *Shining with the Shiner* (a book by John Alexander Lee that followed the story of a man who tramped the country from end to end), or just some other guy who used the name.

I remember one story involved Shiner going to the pub with a clay jug and having the barman fill it up with his favourite whisky. He said: 'Put it on my tab.' The barman said, 'You don't have a tab – pour that whisky out!' And he did, but what the barman didn't realise is that inside was a sponge that he'd haul out later and suck on. Then he'd repeat the scam at the next pub, and so on, until he was quite merry.

There was a 'Pete the Poet' who talked in a poetic flow, using rhyme and blank verse. And another fella whose name escapes me who used to sing in a deep baritone while he walked. The countryside was pretty quiet in the 1950s; there'd be the odd chicken clucking, a dog barking maybe, but otherwise it was near silent, so you could hear this singing from miles away. That wonderful voice! Mum would get the scones on and a pot of tea going whenever she heard it.

They'd tell me about where they'd been and what they'd seen. Sunsets featured a lot – west coast ones in particular. And storms, beautiful streams, good farm country, and kind people. While they talked, they constantly whittled, fashioning spoons, implements and figurines.

They'd talk about the best places to grow crops – corn did well in this place, pumpkin grew well there, kūmara somewhere else. Some of them had gardening tools stashed near their plots. They'd plant near roads on north-facing slopes sheltered from winds, back from the dunes. Occasionally, they spoke about the South Island, which to me as a kid was a distant and fabled land.

You can draw a direct line between five-year-old me listening to swaggers' tall tales and my later wanderings as an adult. The simplicity and apparent freedom of their lives appealed, and they certainly expanded my sense of the world beyond our district. They seemed to wander vast distances. Now you could probably drive their rounds in a matter of hours, but they would walk for months between their haunts. I thought, 'I'm going to be like them when I grow up.'

Around this same time, an 'uncle', Norm Smith, gave me a topographical inch-to-the-mile map. It was of the Spenser Mountains, south of Nelson Lakes. Combined with my experiences of the swaggers, that map did it for me, and I've still got it. Even though I couldn't read or write, I could understand the three-dimensional aspect. I could *read* it, see those orange contour lines and know what that country looked and felt like.

On this particular map, the contour lines suddenly stopped, replaced by blank spaces and the words 'Unexplored Country'. It fascinated me. I could visualise what the landscape did in those blank, unvisited areas based on my reading of the contour lines. Thirty years later when I went to that same area for the first time, it felt like coming home, like stepping into familiar country: 'I know this place; I can read and understand it.' (I've been told on several occasions that a particular edition of an old inch-by-mile map had 'Here be Dragons' instead of 'Unexplored Country'!)

*

One year, the swaggers didn't turn up at the farm. What happened? Did they die? Find another patch? Get a permanent job? Live the rest of their lives in a hut in the bush? Who knows. It just ended. But later when I was at high school, I was coming home on the bus and there was a swagger walking up our road with his pack on his back, billies swinging. When the bus slowed down, I had a chance to look hard at this guy, but I didn't recognise him, and then he fell behind.

It was the last time I saw anyone like him. In the 1960s and early '70s you started to spot adventurers exploring New Zealand on foot, early pioneers of the tramping era. But they had a map and a plan, jobs to get back to and families in the suburbs. It wasn't an all-encompassing lifestyle like it was for the swaggers. The guy I saw from the school bus was the last of his breed, and I was very sad to see him go.

Cobb Hut, Cobb Valley, Kahurangi National Park, 2015.

Chapter 3

On my first day of high school I had to give up bare feet for sandals. But that wasn't the worst part. Moving on to Kaipara College involved a daily bus ride to and from Helensville, and for a while it put a serious crimp in my wanderings.

The good news was that there was a choice of sports, and I was able to opt for harriers. There were only two of us, me and a guy called John Thirkettle, and we'd be let loose every Wednesday afternoon to run through the surrounding countryside. Well, we ran and ran; it was about exploring, not beating the other guy – in fact, John and I made a pact to always cross the finish line side by side. I carried that on later when I joined the air force and ran marathons: they expected me to be out front setting the pace, but I liked to slow down and yarn with the other runners – I really didn't have a competitive bone in my body, much to the annoyance of the organisers.

John and I were supposed to follow a marked trail, but we'd go well beyond that, find a bush-covered valley and duck down into it. Once we were coming down a steep and very muddy hillside and arrived at a farm gate, and John slid under it, then continued running. Well, that was fun – we were 'getting in touch with nature'.

Still, it didn't quite make up for not being able to roam as I used to. Eventually, I began to pretend to my parents that I'd missed the bus home, and I'd run from school to the farm, which was 12 miles by road but only half that distance going across country. I'd shoot over paddocks and through patches of scrub with my school bag slung over my back. As a substitute for exploring it wasn't bad, and it soon became the one aspect of the school day I'd consistently look forward to.

*

Academically, the picture wasn't happy. Until high school, I hadn't really reckoned with my dyslexia. Of course it was a challenge, but I'd always figured that I had other abilities that compensated – the map reading, for example. And lovely Miss Chapple had told me that I had special qualities. My take was: 'Okay, so I can't do this reading thing, but look at all these other skills I've mastered.'

All that went out the window when I got to high school. Suddenly the teachers were dictating lessons, writing long screeds on the blackboard that we were expected to copy. I worked out a few 'hacks'. For dictation, I'd scribble down what I thought was being said, then try to figure it all out when I got home. But it was a holding pattern at best.

Then one day something clicked. It wasn't a single eureka moment, but more a process when things began to come together. Dad helped. He used to tear out articles for me from the *Auckland Weekly* about 'Walking Adventures Down South'. It was considered breaking news back then when eight Aucklanders walked the Milford Track. There were always wonderful photos, and because the images were of such huge interest to me I became more and more keen to try to make sense of the words that went with them. The other big thing I was interested in was aviation. As a young guy I could identify any aircraft that flew by, and because Highway 16 was a navigational route for aircraft flying into Whenuapai I saw plenty. I became increasingly drawn to books about planes.

At 16, I read my first book, *Winnie the Pooh*. It had been given to me as a present many years earlier by a relative, but I hadn't been able to manage it. Now I tried again, but in secret – I didn't want anyone seeing me with a 'kid's book'! Perhaps it was my fascination with the characters and their journeys, including an animal who carries all his worldly possessions tied to the end of a stick; whatever it was, my experience of reading changed with that book.

That was School Certificate year. I failed everything except for woodwork and maths, but got very high marks in both – in fact, I got a national record score for woodwork of 98 per cent! (I still love working with my hands. To me the best materials in the world are old weathered bits of wood, steel and stonework – the building blocks of a backcountry hut. I'm also good with numbers. When I get to a supermarket checkout I'll have already worked out in my head exactly what a shopping trip will cost, which tends to startle the checkout person.) The following year, I repeated School C, scraping through various subjects on my second attempt, but getting great marks for biology and University Entrance maths.

The other thing I did well in at school was a study of 'High-country Farming of the South Island'. Along with those articles from the *Auckland Weekly*, the assignment gave me a taste of that brutal, beautiful southern landscape. What struck me? The huge mountains; the vast tussockland; and the powerful rivers, which seemed so much more impressive than our waterways up north (our Kaipara River was a muddy creek in comparison). It was all so epic and exotic. My pull to the mountains was growing stronger. I started to use the phrase 'The Great Unknown', which was a reference to a place in the headwaters of the Rangitātā River. I'd never been there, of course, but the name exerted a strong fascination.

Kapakapanui Hut, Tararua Range, November 2009.

Chapter 4

In 1970, I left high school and applied to join the air force. Why the air force? Obviously, there was my long fascination with aircraft. One of my very first words was 'plane' – which wouldn't have gone down well with Mum given the trauma she suffered during the Blitz. I was equally obsessed with birds and would become entranced watching a hawk or gull fly.

And there was a family connection. When my father's parents moved to Waimauku, my grandfather worked part-time for the air force at Whenuapai. It was on the RNZAF base that he had the accident that ultimately killed him.

My father had the attitude that 'upstanding citizens' always served their country. I found out after his death that he'd been hugely frustrated that he wasn't allowed to fight in the war. It was for medical reasons – his chest cavity had been damaged during birth and his internal organs were 'disarranged' – but when all his mates from around the district joined the war effort, he shook their hands feeling terribly guilty. (They were all killed, too, so he was lucky – although he never saw it that way.) Instead, he stayed home and helped his widowed mother run the farm – which is where, decades later, he died as an elderly man. He actually dropped dead while moving stock, which for a lifelong farmer must be the ultimate way to go.

Growing up, there was a lot of pressure for someone in the family to 'carry on the tradition', to be a farmer and to be in the military. When it became obvious that I wasn't interested in taking over the farm, my parents felt the next best thing was that I join the air force, with Dad in particular pushing hard.

When you applied for the air force, there was a test you had to sit that basically determined whether you were 'air-crew material' or a plod better suited for ground crew. I'd always had an instinctive aversion to any kind of elitism, and so it immediately put my back up. Rather than try for pilot wings, I went in as an instrument technician, initially training at Wigram, with short courses at Whenuapai and Hobsonville.

My first impressions of the air force were positive. I'd grown up in a small, sheltered community, and I enjoyed meeting people from all over and hearing their stories of other parts of the country. Initially, too, I liked the feeling of being part of a larger group – an 'insider' for once. But that didn't last long.

The air force in the 1970s had a strong macho drinking culture. Guys would start getting pissed at the airmen's club after work on Friday and they'd stay drunk through to Monday morning. These days I enjoy the odd beer at my local pub, the Mussel Inn, but back then I was an abstainer and it immediately set me apart. Likewise with smoking. Every bugger smoked in the 1970s, and we were all given five minutes off each hour to blaze up. I figured I'd keep working and take the cumulative time for a jog around lunch. Again, it marked me out as a bit strange. Doesn't drink? Won't smoke? Likes jogging? What's wrong with the guy? The commanding officer even pulled me aside. 'Look here, Kilgour, why don't you associate more with your fellow airmen?' When I told him I wasn't into wrecking my body with booze and cigarettes he got very steamed up – he was a chain-smoker and loved a drink: 'How dare you criticise the word of a superior officer!'

The work was a good distraction. This was the pre-digitial, pre-electronic instrumentation era, when an altimeter was essentially a modified barometer, and I became fascinated by those simple, straightforward physical instruments. We used to simulate an altitude of 50,000 feet in a pressure chamber to put them through their paces. I remember opening the chamber door once after 24 hours of testing and a blowfly flew out. That fly had been living at 50,000 feet for a whole day and just carried on as normal. What an amazing creature!

Joining the air force was touted as a way to see the world. Personally, I was excited just to be seeing the South Island! I can vividly remember that trip south to Wigram, catching the train to Wellington, followed by the overnight ferry to Lyttelton, and waking up in Lyttelton Harbour. I went up on deck and gazed for a very long time at the Port Hills skyline. Even the foothills appeared impressive.

Then later, when our train came out of the tunnel and I looked across the Canterbury Plains and saw the snow-covered Southern Alps – what a feeling! I'd been influenced by the swaggers, by all my maps and my walking, but this was a new chapter. I thought, 'I'm almost there!' And by that I didn't mean almost at Wigram, or almost about to begin a new job. I meant something deeper.

Pinchgut Hut, North Canterbury.

Chapter 5

At the air-force base, there was a group called the Wigram Outdoor Activity Club, which I quickly joined. Our first day trip – my first-ever tramping trip – was to Mt Richardson, a 1047-metre summit north-west of Christchurch in the Mt Thomas Forest Conservation Area. I put on my boots, shorts, bush singlet and oilskin, and walked into unknown country on a rough bush track.

Most of the group was more interested in getting the walking over and done with so they could head to the Oxford pub. But there was one guy, Steve, who was more on my wavelength who told me he was planning an overnight tramp with a mate up the braided Waimakariri River to the White River Hut in Arthur's Pass National Park. Would I like to come? It took me about a second to say yes.

The following weekend the three of us set out in Steve's two-door Morris 1000. When we got to Porters Pass there was snow everywhere, and the car wasn't handling it well, so Manfred and I stood on the back bumper to add some weight. Up and over we roared, the Morrie fishtailing in the snow and ice.

We parked near the Klondyke Bridge and shouldered our overnight packs – the first of several firsts for me that day. I'd never walked up one of those massive South Island braided river valleys before, never even got my boots wet crossing a river. I soon learned that the only way to warm up properly afterwards was to keep walking. And it was cold, alright, snow down to well below the bushline, the crunch of frost underfoot.

The mountains were extraordinary, steep-sided and much closer than I'd imagined. I felt totally embraced. But it was the beech trees – another first – that I fell in love with. I'd seen pictures of beech forest, but in real life, with the morning sun striking the leaves, it was surprisingly varied. Where I grew up was all plantation pine forest, straight rows, uniform trees. Here there was mountain beech, red beech, black beech – each variety beautiful in its own right, each tree unique.

Although Wigram was out in the countryside, you couldn't escape the whiff of aircraft fuel and cars. Here in the mountains there was none of that, just the earthy fragrance of beech trees and the sandalwood-like scent of subalpine plants. Man, it was gorgeous. Even now when I'm in the mountains and get a sniff of alpine vegetation my head goes straight back to that first overnight tramp.

As we moved further up the valley I spied my first backcountry hut. It was a derelict thing, partly engulfed by a scree slide, but I found it fascinating and lingered for a while. 'The stories this hut could tell!' Finally, we rounded a corner and I saw the White River Hut itself, a little four-bunker set below the park's highest peaks.

As a kid I'd been fascinated by the whare I came across in the North Auckland backblocks, and by swaggers' stories of wandering the backcountry; I'd pored over pictures of South Island rivers and mountains. Now all of that was coming together in one place. It hit me like déjà vu. I thought, 'Wow, this is it! This is *it!*'

Steve had grown up tramping with his grandfather and father, and he now did something that I haven't seen since, but which he said was a tradition. As soon as we got inside the hut, he opened the vermin-proof cupboard, took out food for us to cook, and replaced it with what we'd brought in our packs. That's what trampers used to do back then – leave fresh food for the next party. Another ritual was the fire, which we carefully re-laid for the next person before we left. Those little acts of thoughtfulness caught my imagination. Today we'd probably describe it as 'paying it forward', but back then it was simply part of tramping culture.

That night I had one of the deepest sleeps of my life. And in the morning, another first: toileting in the mountains. Squatting behind a matagouri bush, I saw the sun strike a perfect snow crystal, then spread out across the frost-white ground.

By the time we got back to the Morrie it must have been obvious how excited I was because Steve invited me along for another tramp the next weekend.

This one was a circuit trip, up the Poulter River to the new Casey Hut, then the next day over a saddle to Hallelujah Flat and down the Andrews Stream. It was a rinse and repeat of the White River experience – frosty mornings, sunny days and snow on the ground. Three weekends, three tramps – I was on a roll.

But the Poulter River trip turned out to be my last at Wigram. I learned that I was being sent to Woodbourne base, near Blenheim, to train as an airframe mechanic and fitter – in civilian terms, an aircraft engineer. I left Christchurch soon after on a low-flying Bristol Freighter. There were glass panels in the underside of the nose, and someone had left a mattress there so that you could lie on your stomach and stare down at the terrain. It was a beautiful clear day, and we flew right among the mountains, including very close to mighty Mt Tapuae-o-Uenuku in the inland Kaikōura Range. It was a wonderful introduction to Marlborough, all mountains and sheep country and not a grapevine to be seen.

At Woodbourne, I was assigned to do inflight tests on the aircraft equipment. The test pilot and I became friends, even though he was an officer and I was 'just an airman'. We did a lot of tramping, cycling and running together. His name was Paul Gazley.

The test flights Paul and I did only took us five minutes, but we'd always log the flight as an hour, and for the rest of the time he'd give me flying lessons, or we'd scout out terrain for our next tramping trip or perform some acrobatics. Once we flew upside down over the summit of Tapuae-o-Uenuku in an old Harvard, a single-engine trainer that's been used as a stand-in for Japanese Zeros in movies. Those flights were the highlight of my air-force career, and I took as many of them as I could. At lunch breaks I'd walk across to the airfield, find the commanding officer and ask if I could go for a flight in a Hercules or some other plane.

Did I think of becoming a pilot? It came and went. I was doing a lot of light aircraft flying with friends at the recreational club. Given the number of trial flights I've done, I'd probably be a quite experienced pilot by now. But there was a snobbiness about recreational flying that I couldn't relate to. The guys I flew with were pretty down to earth, but others had a real attitude: 'Oh, and what do *you* fly? And how many hours' flying time have *you* got?' So I didn't pursue it, and later, after I left the air force, I simply couldn't afford to. But I still enjoy going up with friends, and I've never lost my love of aircraft.

Meanwhile, I'd joined the Marlborough Tramping Club. It had about 40 members. Half of us were regular walkers, a quarter joined for the occasional trip and the rest were just interested in the social evenings. There were men and women, school kids, 20-somethings, young families –

people from all walks of life. We had a genuine camaraderie, and did all sorts of things together. The reports we wrote for the tramping club newsletter were called 'Meandering with Marlborough Mates'.

My very first tramp with the club was a three-dayer over the Abel Tasman Inland Track to Awaroa, and then along the coastal track to Mārahau. It was Labour Weekend, 1972. A couple of things will date it for you. The first was that the *Marlborough Express* reported our trip in great detail – I've still got a copy of the article, complete with a photo of me. The second is that throughout those three days we met precisely two other people. Hard to imagine now, but in the early '70s the Abel Tasman qualified as a wilderness experience.

Funnily enough, I knew the two people we bumped into at Awaroa Estuary. One was Max White, who had lived just up the road from where I grew up, and the other was Ross Clark, who lived in nearby Kaukapakapa and whose family knew mine. In the late 1950s and early '60s, Max had been the first Lands and Survey Department Park Ranger based at Tōtaranui, and he was on a bit of a nostalgia trip. They joined us for the coastal section and Max shared inside stories of the park's history.

This was the early tramping era, so we're talking woollen bush shirts and heavy leather boots, basic frame Mountain Mule packs, and Fairydown sleeping bags. Sleeping mats were a rarity; instead, we'd use ferns or a piece of plastic and sleep under a tent fly – in all weather. No one seemed to carry water bottles – there was always plenty of clean water on the route – and we all knew how to make a fire whatever the conditions. Bushcraft was prized and respected.

These were also the days when the New Zealand Forest Service managed game control in the hills and owned all the huts. To go tramping we had to get written permission from the NZFS, which required signatures from any private property owner whose land we planned to cross. It was frustratingly bureaucratic at times. We'd finish one trip and I'd have to start organising a permit for the next.

We were a pretty active bunch. One year I did 54 trips! The bulk were in the Richmond Range because it was so easy to get to from Blenheim – you could potentially even cycle there after work – with relatively easy access to the ridges and tops, and a basic hut every three or four hours.

About a year after I joined the Marlborough Tramping Club, I did a trip to Tongariro/Ngāuruhoe with Ross, who'd become a member of the Marlborough Tramping Club despite living near Auckland. After downing tools for the week, I took the air-force 'shuttle aircraft' to Wellington, then an overnight train to National Park station that arrived around 1 am. The station master allowed me to kip in his office, asking me to lock up when I left. So trusting! Ross and his friends, a brother and sister, arrived at the station the next morning.

We walked what is now the Tongariro Crossing and saw virtually no one in three days. The volcanic plateau was strange and beautiful, twin cones rising from vast rocky country, steam venting dramatically from Ngāuruhoe and the pungent smell of sulphur. I'd read about this part of the North Island, but to be standing atop an active volcano was something else. It was Easter and the only snow visible was on Ruapehu in the distance. We walked down the other side of the mountains to the 1904 Waihohonu Hut, which was once used as a stopover for tourist stagecoaches, and is now a museum piece. In the 1970s it was literally the only place to stay. As one of the very first huts I bagged, it was memorable for its unique insulation – an infill of pumice gathered from the surrounding landscape and packed into the cavity between internal and external corrugated-iron walls.

*

As I became more of a fixture at the club, I took on something of a guardian's role with some of the younger members. The first was a high-school lad, Russell Sanders, who sadly died in Perth the year before I wrote this. He and his parents and siblings were involved in a lot of the club tramps, and they asked me if it was okay for Russell to come along on some of my walks. There was another high-schooler, Russell Montgomery, who later became a park ranger. His mother had just died and his father said to me, 'Russell is taking it particularly hard. I know tramping would be good for him, but because I'm so busy with all of his siblings I don't have time. Would you take him?' The third member of our little group was Lana, who was in her late teens and had a job as a gardener for the local council. We called ourselves the 'Rustlers' in honour of the two youngest.

We took a week-long trip in the Richmond Range in the middle of winter once. There are pictures of us surrounded by snow on top of Mt Richmond, all wearing the classic bush shirt, shorts and big boots, holding ice axes. We'd travel vast distances, often through unmarked territory. One time it got very stormy and we had to bail out down the Maitai Valley and into Nelson then hitch a ride back to Blenheim in a big-rig truck.

We travelled up the Waihopai Valley, too, into the Bounds Range. Mt Bounds and Pinnacle are the dominant peaks there, while the major rivers are the Waihopai, the Branch, the Leatham and the Wye. Off the Waihopai was the Gosling Stream, where the tramping club had a hut. It was just a basic thing with walls and a roof, but we slowly clad it and put in a floor and a fireplace. We used it as a base to climb Mt Bounds or head up the Leatham River and Boulder Stream to Mt Pinnacle.

Pinnacle was well-named – it's not much more than a pointed top, and stands at 6991 feet. The Rustlers climbed it in winter and when we got to the summit, Lana announced that she wanted to stick her hand through 7000 feet. We put her on our shoulders and she stretched up and made it. I once told this to a writer who translated it into metric in the article – which kind of missed the point!

In those early days, there was a strong fitness motivation to tramping – to all my outdoor activity, really. And I'd think nothing of cycling for three or four hours after finishing work on a Friday, doing some serious tramping on the weekend, then getting back to the base five minutes before work started again on Monday.

Being super-fit felt fantastic. When walking, I'd get into a real rhythm, aware of my breathing, my stride, pace, heartbeat – a state where everything lined up and I began to feel that I could walk forever. I tried to describe this zone once in a speech at a tramping club evening and an old guy down the back yelled out: 'I know *exactly* what you mean!' It's so inspiring to experience that energy, to appreciate just how much potential the human body has. I think about that when I get blue sometimes. That potential's still there. I'm nearly 70, but it's still there.

I cycled vast distances when I was at Woodbourne. On Friday afternoons, I'd bike up the Wairau Valley to Nelson Lakes, park my bike off the side of a track and go tramping in the night. I'd get halfway up the Travis Valley and have a sleep, then head over the Travis Saddle, down the Sabine, over to Lake Angelus. On Sunday evening, after it'd gone dark, I'd cycle back to Blenheim, buzzing.

Sometimes, there were others from the club with me, and we'd tramp in the dark singing our heads off. A couple of women I knew from Blenheim once told me they'd been camping just off the track and heard us yodelling as we walked past. If we could force ourselves to be quiet for any length of time, we'd sometimes hear kiwi calling – a far more pleasant tune!

I loved walking at night for the atmosphere. One of the regulars had an old carbide lantern left over from the mining days, which hissed and smelt horrible, but threw some terrific shadows. The rest of us carried powerful Dolphin torches. These old-school Dolphins with their massive batteries were ridiculously heavy; today it's all about travelling light. The other great thing about night-tramping was the effect on your non-visual senses. Beech forest never smelled so good as it did walking through it in darkness.

For my annual leave, I'd take two weeks off to visit my parents. Friday afternoon there was always a light air-force aircraft going over to Wellington, and I would catch a lift with my bike, then cycle to the Wellington Railway Station to see where the next train was heading. If it was Paekākāriki or Masterton I'd take it, then start cycling north, riding through the night. When I got tired, I'd scout out a spot on the side of the road, pull out my sleeping mat and have a cat-nap, then carry on. Sometimes I'd head straight up the main highway – these days you'd be taking your life in your hands doing that – but mostly I took backroads.

I recall cycling through Henderson in West Auckland at 3 am on one trip, not a person to be seen, then arriving at my parents' early that morning as naturally high as a kite. It was wonderful. At the end of the two weeks, I cycled the 20-odd kilometres to Whenuapai and caught a Bristol Freighter back to Woodbourne.

Old Crow Hut, Karamea River.

Chapter 6

By now my outdoor skills were well honed. I could read the bush, tramp as long as I needed to, and was comfortable with unmarked routes. Perhaps, I thought, I should use my new knowledge to help people.

Initially, I joined the Woodbourne air-force Search and Rescue squad, then signed up as a volunteer for the tramping-club equivalent. There was a bit of a weird hierarchy thing going on in the air-force team, with very young, sometimes even teenaged officers in charge of experienced backcountry men. These kids had learned the lingo, done the schooling, but they were lacking in practical smarts. The club team was much more my cup of tea – pragmatic, down to earth and focused on getting into the hills and learning new skills rather than playing bullshit games.

With both teams we did plenty of exercises and saw relatively little action – a bit like that saying about war being long periods of boredom punctuated by short moments of excitement. But Marlborough during winter was a great place to learn alpine skills without having to travel too far. We'd head up Mt Bounds and practise climbing skills such as rope work, belaying and self-arresting techniques on varying degrees of ice slopes from gentle to almost overhanging.

The air-force exercises were always a major performance. We'd have to carry in massive tents, but our food supplies would be airdropped. That could be entertaining. I recall one trip when Paul Gazley had to fly in a food drop in atrocious weather. We were in the Waiau Valley under thick clouds and could hear him making pass after pass in his Devon aircraft, looking for a safe way through. Finally, he just went for it and flew in at barely 50 metres to drop the load. Unfortunately, you need at least 100 metres for a parachute to open, so this food drop hurtled down and buried itself in the ground. There was a brief moment of cheering, before the hole started filling with a frothing amber-coloured liquid. The beer! I'd never seen so many grown men close to tears. Thankfully, my cans of fruit juice were intact.

Another winter exercise that went a little off the rails took place at Dip Flat, up the Wairau Valley. It was winter and the backroads were pretty icy. Our Land Rover left the road at a corner, plummeted 20 metres or so, and came to a violent halt among beech trees. We were all shaken but uninjured, so we climbed out, thinking we'd unroll the winch at the front, run it up to the top and haul the vehicle back up to the road. Only, the winch was totally frozen. Someone said, 'I know, we'll all piss on it! But let's drink the booze first!' And someone else said, 'Nah, it's too early in the day; let's boil the billy and have some coffee and then take a piss on it.' So we boiled the billy, at which point someone sharper than the rest had an idea: 'We've got hot water, so why not just pour that on the winch!' A bloody genius!

When we did get call-outs, they could be emotionally brutal. I remember an early search for two elderly men who had disappeared while fishing from a rowboat in the Marlborough Sounds. One had had a heart attack and was found in the sea still hanging on to his fishing line with a large snapper hooked. The other had made it ashore and tried to climb a rock, but had fallen and hit his head and died.

During the search someone found some false teeth and called on the radio asking what to do with them. He was told to put them in his pocket, but to 'be careful that they don't bite!' Insensitive maybe, but in those situations a bit of black humour sometimes helps.

Another event involved a farmer who hadn't returned from going up a river valley with his horse and dogs to muster sheep. This was in the days before beacons and mobile phones. Four teams were involved in that search: police, air force and reluctantly invited tramping club and Deerstalkers Association posses.

Well, the first two groups were absolutely useless. The deerstalkers got to the farmer first, and we trampers arrived ten minutes later. He'd been leading his horse across a stream when it had jumped, and in the fall he'd broken both his legs. We stretchered him for two or three hours. About half an hour from the vehicles, the police and air-force guys finally appeared, coming the other way, and tried to take over, but the farmer insisted we carry him out. Even so, the headline in the next day's newspaper was 'Police Save Injured Farmer'. We didn't want any glory, but still it stuck in the craw.

*

Search and Rescue in the twenty-first century is a very different beast. For a start, it's viewed as a team effort – no one is a hero. Also, they concentrate far more these days on the psychological aspect, working up profiles of the missing person, their state of mind and character traits. In 2020, I was asked to help narrow the search for two 20-something trampers who went missing in the Kahurangi National Park. The first thing the SAR team asked me was 'What's your gut feeling?' We knew this pair didn't have maps or compasses with them. I thought it was likely they would have got onto a ridge and got confused about direction. If the weather was poor, they would have climbed down into a gully.

The SAR guys were also interested in my close knowledge of the terrain. What were the gullies like? The creeks? I described a mix of thick bush and scratchy, impenetrable subalpine vegetation, and told them there was also massive amounts of windfall in the area from an earlier tropical cyclone. Hundreds of old rimu and tōtara had had their tops snapped off and been scattered like broken spars. I'm not sure if my contribution helped, but I was sure relieved when the trampers were found.

I had a more personal experience of the modern SAR approach when a friend went missing on one of our tramps. It was a day trip with three mates from the Cobb powerhouse up to the Kill Devil Pack Track, following an unofficial route marked with rags. The idea was to walk for half a day, then one of us would backtrack to get our vehicle and drive to the end of the track while the rest carried on. But when we arrived at the end, our friend who'd gone for the car wasn't there. A farmer offered us his ute to drive back to the powerhouse, where we found the car still parked. Using the emergency phone at the Cobb power station we rang the police and the missing guy's wife, and eventually searchers arrived.

The SAR guys interviewed me closely to build up a profile. Among other things, they asked me what annoyed me most about my mate. I said he could be stubborn and impatient. It was all added to the mix to figure out how he might be thinking.

When they found him by helicopter the next day, we learned that he'd gone off a ridge thinking that he was on the left side when he was actually on the right. I could just envisage him trying to convince himself: 'No, I'm sure I'm correct! Gotta keep moving.' I have an old mountain safety brochure on what to do if you are lost. It says: 'Stop. Make a cup of tea. Relax. Think about it.' My mate was impatient, trying to make his surroundings fit with his theory rather than pause and problem-solve.

*

Why do people get lost? I reckon a lot of people get thrown by fear. They get confused about where they are, then panic. It clouds their ability to make good decisions. On the flipside, a lot of people are overconfident about their abilities in the great outdoors, and often that's combined with stubbornness.

Overconfidence can push people over the edge. Like that young guy a few years ago who was trying to travel super-lightweight through the New Zealand backcountry; he fell on a bluff and was found dead, after surviving the initial fall and getting into his sleeping bag. That case inspired me to start taking a locator beacon whenever I go tramping (along with my trusty old NZMS 260 maps and an older eTrex GPS). I'm aware, however, that beacons can lull people into false confidence. They think they can go anywhere with no cares or worries. But do they know how to use their beacons? Do they check them? Two years ago, a guy asked me for advice about climbing a particular mountain. I told him to take an hour or two longer and go around the easiest ridges. Instead, he chose a shortcut, fell and was badly injured. He had to wait 24 hours to be rescued after his beacon was thrown from his bag during the fall.

I've been lost in the backcountry. One time in Australia could have been serious – I'll get to that episode a bit later.

In New Zealand, there's been the odd occasion when I've been 'momentarily geographically embarrassed'. There was a solo trip in Marlborough when I followed a creek off the Leatham Valley and arrived at the tops just as it started snowing. I ended up on a side track that took me to the head of the Waihopai Valley. Those were the pre-GPS days when you relied heavily on your trusty inch-to-the-mile map, and using a compass and working hard to keep the map dry in atrocious weather, I figured it out. Was I truly lost? I knew where I was, but it certainly wasn't where I intended to be.

Kirwans Hut, West Coast.

Chapter 7

For a period in the mid-1970s I became absorbed with a new challenge: technical mountaineering. I'd caught the bug during wintertime SAR exercises, where we focused on rock- and ice-climbing and snow work.

In '74 I headed down to Mt Cook with half a dozen other adventure-minded members of the tramping club to do a week-long alpine skills course with professional guides. The Rustlers came along, and an 'old fella' – he was probably about 40 at the time – we'd adopted called Tony Hendry, who had just lost his wife. (As an aside, Tony is now 96, and when he turned 90 he said, 'I just want to let everybody know I've given up running the Buller half-marathon – I'm going to walk it instead.') The course was guided by Gavin Wills, founder of Alpine Guides.

In those days, the approach was more casual. We didn't have to sign endless waivers as you do now, and the cost for a week was reasonable. And mountaineering itself was far less technical. Most of us were still climbing with basic crampons and an ice axe; there was none of this modern specialist kit. We wore our normal tramping clothes, the thick bush singlets and bush shirts, Swanndri, oilskin coats and heavy boots.

We did the training up in the Kitchener Range behind Mt Cook Village, practising snow and ice travel, ice-face and rock-climbing, a lot of ropework, belaying and bivvying in rock on the edge of the snow. We had dabbled with some of this in Marlborough, read the 'Safety in the Mountains' booklets and so on, but we learned a heck of a lot more up on Mt Kitchener.

Three years later we all returned to Mt Cook for a follow-up intermediate alpine skills course, where we took things to the next level. It was run by Max Dorfliger, a Swiss-born alpinist who'd been nicknamed 'Maxi the Taxi' because of the huge packs he'd carry around the place. In the 1970s, Max became the first person to solo climb the Caroline Face on Aoraki/Mt Cook, and he was a terrific guide for us. He and I have stayed in touch ever since. These days he's heavily involved in tramping-hut restoration work in the Arthur's Pass area, and is just as precise and clever a carpenter as he was a mountaineer. Max really took a shine to our group, and at the end of the course he offered to spend a second week with us putting our new skills into action, culminating in an ascent of Mt Elie de Beaumont, the towering 3109-metre peak at the head of the Tasman Glacier.

The previous day we'd spent hours staring up at this intimidating mountain from outside the Tasman Saddle Hut, using compass and altimeter to suss out a route to take us safely up the main face between crevasses. At 3 am sharp, we put on our cramponed boots and left the hut. There were six of us, roped in pairs, moving one at a time and applying what we'd learned on the course. In places the slope went well past 45 degrees, and occasionally we'd have to use our ice axes to cut steps. It was hard graft and required total focus on each task – you couldn't let your thoughts drift to 'what ifs', such as what if I fell off the edge right now? In any case, I had confidence from our training. We'd practised spontaneous slips, how to arrest your fall and how to belay quickly to stop someone sliding off the mountain, and I think we all felt we could trust the person at the other end of the rope. And because it was so early in the day, the snow and ice underfoot was still stable, with no soft patches that could potentially become avalanches. Despite it being such a grunt, I felt elated to be high among the peaks in the darkness.

And then suddenly we were at the summit. After a rest, we boiled some billy tea, Max broke out a celebratory box of chocolates, and we drank and ate as the sun came up. It was a magnificent scene. To the east was a carpet of cloud through which other high peaks poked, and you felt you could almost walk to them. Then as the cloud started to disperse the sun broke through and lit everything up, the colours shifting from deep charcoal to bruised purple to red to pink, with the shadow of Elie de Beaumont casting a dark pyramid over the Tasman Sea. It was hard to tear ourselves away, but after an hour at the top we roped up for the descent.

It was just as well we didn't stay longer, because that first hour of sunshine had already started to soften the snow dangerously, and as we stepped down we set off a number of small avalanches. That's when you realise that reaching the summit isn't the end of things – the prize in mountaineering is to make a safe descent.

*

Summiting Elie de Beaumont was easily the highlight of my brief mountaineering career; it was also the beginning of the end. Afterwards I climbed other peaks with various people in the Nelson Lakes, Arthur's Pass and Marlborough areas, including an ascent of Mt Tapuae-o-Uenuku, but my enthusiasm was waning. The problem was that we were all becoming far too competitive. It was an addictive thing; each climb had to be bigger and better and faster than the one before. We had to 'conquer' new and higher peaks, to 'knock the bastard off'. How quickly could you summit that southern face? Gee, you were a bit slow today. That mindset had never appealed to me. In the air force I'd joined the cross-country team, and it drove the bosses mad when I deliberately slowed to finish alongside the other guys. They got really upset that I wouldn't 'put the hammer down'.

The other thing was that people were starting to die around me. Our SAR team had three Pauls including me, and the other two both died in mountaineering accidents. One fell thousands of feet from Mt Angelus into the Hopeless Valley; the other, who died in an avalanche on the Ball Glacier in 1975, was my good mate, the pilot Paul Gazley.

Paul Gazley had previously survived being buried for 12 hours by an avalanche just off Aoraki/Mt Cook – actually, he was working on an article about the experience for the alpine club magazine when he died. It was a Search and Rescue exercise, an air-force party of 27. Eight of them were swept away; four were badly injured and four died. I was supposed to be with them, but had had to withdraw the day before when an urgent job came up. (I had other near misses. In 1977, I got held up in the Haast/King Memorial Hut in Aoraki/Mt Cook National Park by the most horrific storm I've ever known. It blew away part of the hut, the awnings and even the long drop. That same storm hit Three Johns Hut nearby and blew it clean off the Barron Saddle, killing four hikers. One of them, a young doctor named Fenella Druce, was memorialised in the naming of Fenella Hut in the Cobb Valley.)

Paul's death was a turning point. I was still figuring out what kind of person I wanted to be and where my path lay, but I knew that 'conquering' peaks wasn't part of it. Once you have a taste of the bush and the mountains and start to appreciate your relationship with them, you hopefully develop some humility. From my point of view, we were there on the mountains' terms, not to try to beat them. They were serene and beautiful places and I was just thankful to be there.

*

Around the time I was falling out of love with mountaineering, I quit the air force. For a couple of years I'd been asking myself, 'What am I doing this for?' It was financing my tramping trips, but that was about it. I realised, 'Hell, I'm doing this for my parents!' Their friends would always tell me how proud my folks were to have a son in uniform, but I was starting to chafe under those expectations.

There were plenty of things about the air force I wasn't happy about. Every year we would head to the rifle range and fire off 200 rounds, and I enjoyed that. But one year we arrived at the range and they'd changed all the targets to life-sized images of men with Asian features charging out of the jungle – a Vietnam thing. When I said, 'I'm not going to shoot at an image of a person', the officer in charge told me he'd 'stick this f**king bayonet' up me if I didn't shoot. I deliberately fired to miss. He said, 'So you're a conchie are ya?' and marched me to the commanding officer.

The CO was an Englishman, Tony West. He asked me whether I wanted a cup of tea, then spoke. 'It's very good to be honest with your own feelings,' he said. I thought, 'Am I really hearing this?' He called in the padre, who reiterated how important it was to follow your conscience, then wrote me an exemption from shooting.

(A few years later while cycling around the South Island I found myself at Todds Valley near Nelson. Someone told me that down the valley an older retired couple were growing organic veges on a block of land, and they were welcoming young people to stay and learn from them. Well, it turned out to be Tony West! He'd left the air force to set up one of Nelson's first alternative lifestyle communities. We had a good laugh about the target-shooting controversy.)

The corporal involved in that incident was a little pot-bellied fella, and he loved yelling. When he yelled his cheeks would go bright red, his nose even redder. Once, he walked up to me on the parade ground, held his baton hard under my nose and said, 'At the end of this stick is a fucking wanker.' I replied, 'Which end?' The entire parade ground burst into laughter, and he started running around, waving his stick, his nose getting redder and redder. Once again, I was marched off to see the commanding officer – Tony again – who thought it was hilarious. I can laugh now, too, but at the time it reinforced my feeling that I needed to quit. Surely there was more for me in life than being screamed at by red-faced corporals?

The other thing that I didn't enjoy was the snobbery. At lunchtime I used to do a four-and-a-half-mile jog around the airfield that cut across the front lawn of the officers' mess. One time an officer bailed me up and asked what the hell I thought I was doing on his part of the base? 'You're just an airman!' A friend and I used to bait this young officer, who was constantly trying to find fault with the lower ranks. We'd walk around with our hats off and pretend not to see him when he started making a fuss. It was a silly them-versus-us game, and I became weary of it.

So I was itching to leave. The problem was that when I'd signed on I'd bound myself to the air force for a certain number of years – ten, from memory. You could plead a case, but it was a major process. You couldn't just quit; you might even have to do something terrible to get yourself booted out.

But by this stage of the '70s there were so many people disillusioned with the military that the authorities introduced a change. I learned that there was a form that allowed you to exit without having to explain why or to argue special circumstances. I signed in October 1976 and was gone by December.

I'd worried about my parents' reaction, and it wasn't good. They took a long time to get over it. My grandfather never did, which was sad. But I didn't look back. Not long after handing in my uniform, I was on a plane to Sydney, and from there, via Bangkok then Calcutta, to Nepal.

The old Devils Creek Hut, Mt Richmond Forest Park.

Chapter 8

As a kid I'd been fascinated by Edmund Hillary's mountaineering. As an adult, it was his work with the Sherpa people that got me. I was eager to see the Himalayas in all their glory, but I also wanted to immerse myself in the place and meet people.

But first I needed to get used to my new surrounds. After the sheltered upbringing of a dairy farm north of Auckland followed by the all-enveloping world of the air force, to suddenly find myself alone on the streets of Kathmandu was quite the culture shock. I hired a bike and went everywhere, up all the side alleys, soaking in the sounds and smells of the place. I witnessed a group of local people fighting each other to get a plastic bag that was blowing along the street.

I chose to trek what is now the main tourist drag, the route to Everest Base Camp. From Kathmandu I took the daily bus service in the direction of the Tibetan border, a local bus with chickens in coops strapped to the roof and every seat taken. After a couple of hours, the driver pulled to a stop and waved for me to get off. It took me a while to register that this was the start of the trail. The only indication was a rough handwritten sign on a fencepost, beyond which a narrow track disappeared into scrubby vegetation. There was no information about distances, landmarks – not even an arrow! Which way to Lukla? To Namche Bazaar?

I saw virtually no other hikers, but plenty of locals going about their business. One day I came around a corner and found a crowd praying and weeping. A group had been doing track work when a 12-year-old boy among them had tumbled off a cliff and disappeared into the river below. Well, their prayers were answered, because he eventually re-emerged, grabbed a pick and started working again!

The scale of the Nepalese landscape struck me dumb. The mountains were monumental, of course, dwarfing anything I'd experienced at Aoraki/Mt Cook, but so was everything. You'd come across a river valley in the morning and not get close to reaching the far side until the end of the day. And it was epically beautiful. When I was there the rhododendron forest was in bloom, and everywhere the distant alps were foregrounded by bursts of bright pink and red. At the same time, every inch of productive country was intensively cropped. The people I met were subsistence farmers, their whole lives revolving around the mountains and the weather, and they were totally tuned in to their surroundings.

I travelled light – my Mountain Mule pack, a change of clothes and an Everest sleeping bag, but no tent. Occasionally I slept under the stars, but mostly I stayed in teahouses along the route. These places were pretty basic but built strongly of stone with slate on the roof, and they were often colourfully decorated. Invariably there was a fire burning, but with no chimneys the smoke had to try to find a way out through the cracks. In the lower country they burned wood, but as you got up higher in the mountains it was dried yak dung, which had a distinctive sweet scent. For a dollar I'd get a roof over my head at the end of a long day of walking, a filling meal of rice or dahl with occasionally a bit of chicken thrown in, and as many cups of the local 'yak butter' tea as I could handle. It was a sweet broth-like concoction made using butter, sugar and great handfuls of tea leaves boiled like mad, and I developed a real taste for it.

I always got a warm and generous welcome in Nepal. It was the typical story: people who at first glance seem to be living with so little are often the most generous and open. The kids were intrigued by me. I was sporting my first-ever beard and with my air-force crewcut growing out I must have cut a raggedy figure. And I was wearing shorts! They'd run up and touch my hairy legs and laugh.

In the high country, I came across my first Ed Hillary-built school and learned the power of the Kiwi connection. 'Where are you from?' 'From New Zealand.' 'Oh, please come in!' The teacher told the class where I was from, and a kid ran off and returned with pictures of Sir Ed and other New Zealanders they'd met – some of whom I knew from tramping! I found it moving to see how much a Kiwi had helped them. Other countries gave aid, but it always came with strings. Hillary said, 'What do you need and how do you want it?' and he delivered. Throughout the trip, I was given letters to take back for 'Mr Ed Mund, New Zealand'. I sent them on when I got home, and received a lovely letter of thanks from Sir Ed.

In the Nepalese high country, altitude sickness is always a risk. I'd heard about 'basket cases' – foreign hikers who had to be carried down from the danger zone in baskets borne on Sherpas' backs. Then in my second week of trekking, I bumped into some Americans who'd lost almost half their tour group to altitude sickness. They'd already paid for a certain number of tents and porters and didn't want to cancel, and they were inviting random hikers to join their party to Base Camp. I tagged along, enjoying both the company and the perks.

Nearing Base Camp, I was feeling like I'd dodged the altitude bullet, that my month-long methodical climb must have acclimatised me, unlike all those fly-in tourists who raced straight up from Lukla Airport. But at 16,000 feet I started to develop the dreaded symptoms: the gasping for air, blinding headaches, and vomiting whenever I ate more than a snack. It was awful.

I was told about a Japanese doctor at a medical centre nearby who was studying how altitude sickness affected the eyes, so I thought I'd volunteer myself to medical science and maybe get some help. When I arrived, however, the first thing I saw was the poor guy writhing on the floor in agony, attended by his worried staff – altitude sickness! That was the end of the eye test for me. Instead, I descended to 14,000 feet, and the trouble vanished. I've since been in other high-altitude environments and the lesson I've absorbed is that it pays to take it slow. Ignore all deadlines and you'll generally get there with your lungs in one piece.

On my way back from Base Camp, I met a Nepalese family who were intending to trek to the Arun Valley, a month's walk away, and they invited me to go with them. I walked through some amazing country, never saw a foreigner, and heard English used exactly once, by a 12-year-old who wanted to practise the language: 'What is the time, please, sir?' and 'Has your beautiful wife borne you many children?' He got such obvious enjoyment from saying the words. In the end I spent four months in Nepal, well and truly overstaying my visa.

I'd left the air force and New Zealand because I'd sensed that there was a more exciting world out there. Walking in the Himalayas confirmed that I'd made the right call. There was no one now to tell me how I should wear my hat or when I should shave – no one to tell me to do anything at all. And I was meeting these incredible people whose lives were so intimately tied to their environment.

It took me ages to absorb what happened in Nepal – to be honest, I'm probably still working on it. It's like they say: travel broadens the mind. On a seminal trip like that, your eyes are opened to what's important. I learned to accept and respect people for who they are; that people who live in the most basic circumstances are usually the most generous; that they tend to focus on the here and now, on what is needed to survive. I'm not sure I could live so austerely, but I still try to keep things as simple, stripped back and in-the-moment as possible.

*

I returned to Blenheim, to the little cottage at Tuamarina where I'd moved after quitting the air force. I had a lot of friends in Marlborough from the tramping club, so it made sense to base myself there while I contemplated my next move.

It was a time when you could easily get fruit-picking or farm work, and I did a lot of that, plus the odd shift in the local dairy factory and a bit of gardening. Later, I visited the Forest Service HQ at Renwick and asked after a job. The boss told me that he didn't have a vacancy but he reckoned he could probably create one for me. The position he came up with involved heading into the hills to check tracks and huts and make observations on goat populations.

I remember wondering how the job could be justified economically, but that was the way the Forest Service operated. They had people on the payroll doing things that made you scratch your head, such as teams employed to plant conifers on mountain scree slopes. That always seemed like a bad idea to me, and I said so, and now we're having to clean up the mess of all those wilding pines.

Mine was a fun job while it lasted. On Monday morning, we'd chopper in supplies to various Marlborough backcountry huts, along with hunters, hut and track workers and pine-tree planters. Once I'd been dropped off, my job was to patrol the track and huts, keeping an eye out for goats, pigs and deer, as well as chamois, which had been sighted in the mountains near the Branch and Leatham rivers. I'd jot the numbers down at the end of my ten-day shift and pass the record on to my boss. To this day I have no idea if it was useful or just a box-ticking exercise to keep the Wellington bean counters happy.

After a year, the role was terminated, but I wasn't too worried. Whenever I emerged from time in the bush, whether it was Kahurangi Park, the Richmond Range or Nelson Lakes, my mind would be clearer and another job would soon present itself. I felt confident that my simple needs would be met.

*

In the summer of 1979, I joined tens of thousands of hippies at the multi-day Nambassa Festival on a farm north of Waihī – my third in three years. Nambassa was our answer to Woodstock, with side helpings of New Age spiritualism, alternative medicine and counterculture art. There were always a few decent acts on stage – Little River Band and Split Enz played that year – but plenty of people went along for the workshops and meditation sessions, or to touch the hem of an Indian swami. I remember Barry McGuire sang

'Eve of Destruction', but then followed up with some preachy Christian folk and was booed off stage. Something like 65,000 people turned up in '79, and it was glorious – although not without controversy.

Nambassa sowed peace, love and harmony – and, unfortunately, several cases of hepatitis. After the festival ended, I stayed on to help with the clean-up of the food-stall area. The place was a mess, bins overflowing, and I've often wondered if that might be when I picked up the illness that derailed my year.

It hit me soon after while I was tramping in the remote west of Rakiura/Stewart Island. I spent a fortnight of walking getting crooker and crooker, my energy draining like water through a bunghole. I wondered what the heck was going on with me. When I reached Doughboy Bay, I had to stop. At the southern end of the bay I found a shallow but dry cave, with a southern rātā overhanging the entrance. A few weeks earlier this cave had been at the centre of a curious news story when a group of deerstalkers discovered a middle-aged Japanese woman living there. Reportedly the wife of a wealthy industrialist, Keiko Agatsuma had arrived in New Zealand on a tourist visa in late 1978, and eventually went off-grid on Stewart Island, surviving on groceries bought in Bluff and pāua prised from the rocks. She was eventually deported back to Japan for overstaying her visa, with no one much the wiser about what drove her to become the 'Japanese woman cave dweller of Stewart Island'.

Keiko had made the cave nice and homely: there were salvaged fishing buoys for decoration, a bed made from a net stretched over boards and a fireplace in a 44-gallon drum. I rested there for two days, gathering strength for the climb over to the Mason Bay Hut. At Freshwater Landing, I met a fisherman who told me that I looked very crook, and offered me a lift out to Halfmoon Bay. Eventually, I got a ride from Christchurch to Blenheim with friends, and arrived home feeling wrecked.

I had an air ticket booked to the United States, and a big adventure planned biking solo across the country from the west coast to the east. But my worried friends persuaded me to see a doctor, who diagnosed severe hepatitis, a notifiable disease. The trip was off, and I was placed in quarantine at a friend's house in Blenheim.

It was a low point for me. At the time, there was a lot of paranoia about hepatitis, and in conservative Blenheim my story was a big thing. The local rag even ran an article about me – it wasn't sympathetic. I felt like a leper. At the same time, I was getting conflicting information from various professionals about how serious it was, from 'You don't need to worry' to 'This is a deadly disease'. I knew I couldn't break quarantine, not even to go bush, and that was brutal on my mental health – the bush had always been where I went for solace. I'd look up at the hills and feel stuck and stymied, and increasingly depressed. To give myself something to look forward to, I booked a treat, a scenic flight to Antarctica on an Air New Zealand DC-10, later that year.

In mid-winter, just as I was starting to feel I might have turned the corner, I got a call. Two tramping mates, Tony Hendry and Jeffrey Parker, were planning an adventure in the Mt Aspiring National Park. I should come, they said, get into the mountains and get myself right. A doctor gave me the all-clear to finish quarantine, but he cautioned me strongly about doing any serious tramping. I needed to allow my body to heal, he warned. But of course I wasn't listening to a word he said. The next day I rang Air New Zealand and cancelled my Antarctica ticket, annoyed that I was charged a $20 cancellation fee!

We all left Blenheim at the same time by different modes – Jeff on his motorbike, Tony on a bus and me hitching – but arrived in Wānaka at the same time. That was a propitious sign. After some hasty planning and gathering of provisions, we made camp under Mt Aspiring in the Matukituki Valley, where I received another good omen. In the middle of the night I was woken by a swishing noise, like fireworks. When I poked my head out of the tent, I couldn't quite believe what I was seeing: a meteor shower. I called out to the others, but they wanted to keep sleeping. To be absolutely sure that I wasn't dreaming, I reached out and touched first snow and then a matagouri bush. One was cold, the other sharp – it was real, alright.

Our route the next day took us up the Matukituki River West Branch, then a steep climb from the valley floor through bush and subalpine tussock to French Ridge Hut. If we'd tramped it six months earlier I would have found it a doddle, but that first day was tough going for me. When you've been through an illness like hepatitis, it takes a long time to recover your former fitness level and reserves of energy. But boy, was it worth the effort. The hut was perched at around 1500 metres, immediately below the snow line and dizzingly high above the Matukituki Valley. My body ached, but my spirits were soaring. The phrase from my very first overnight tramp was ringing in my head – *this is it*!

We'd planned to climb to Colin Todd Hut, right at the toe of Aspiring's north-west ridge, but bad weather thwarted us. Instead, we explored the Makarora River for a few days before Jeff made the call to head home. Tony and I weren't ready to stop, though, so we hitched our way to the Hollyford Valley and walked the Hollyford Track through to Martins Bay and then up the West Coast. Then I headed off solo to check out the Hopkins River Valley on the border of Otago and Canterbury, following my nose up tributaries, having a wonderful time and feeling more and more like my old self. I shot up to Aoraki/Mt Cook National Park for an explore, then headed south to walk the Milford Track. It was the end of 1979, a difficult year for me, but it could have been so much worse. When I emerged from tramping the Milford I learned that an Air New Zealand flight had crashed in Antarctica. I put it together later: it was the flight I'd been booked on.

Makakoere Hut, Te Urewera.

Chapter 9

For years I'd told Mum how keen I was to get to know my Aussie relatives, but she always refused to give me their address. She said they'd be too disappointed in what I'd become. I just had a bit of a beard and long hair! In 1980, I decided I'd fly over anyway. Silas had recently died and left me a bit of money, and I figured he would have approved of using it to go meet his family.

I knew that he'd grown up in a town called Bombala near the Snowy Mountains, so I hitched there. My last lift was with a Bombala local, who told me about a shop in town where a woman, Hermoyne Ferry, worked whose maiden name was Brasington. She turned out to be my mother's cousin, and so began a relationship with my Aussie relatives. Hermoyne's daughter Vivienne, my second cousin, had by chance when travelling stopped at a garage sale, where she found a very old and thick dictionary. In the front in very beautiful handwriting was my grandfather's full name (Silas Augustus Phillip Brasington) and the words 'Happy birthday, son, from father, 1904'. Vivienne gave it to me, and I cherish it – my great-grandfather's actual handwriting! To this day, contacting them is one of the most amazing things I've done – they're all terrific people.

After Bombala, I hitched on to meet my relatives in South Queensland and found that Silas's brother was still alive. He was in his mid-nineties and was blind, but he touched my hair and face and said, 'Oh, that long hair and beard really suits a Brasington!' (When I told my mother she was mortified.)

Roy was his name. One of his arms finished at the elbow, and he only had three fingers, yet he could play the piano and the fiddle. An amazing guy. These relatives were farming people and really laidback. It was wonderful to learn that at least some of my family was broadminded, and that I could relate to them.

From Queensland, I made my way to Tasmania. I walked out of Hobart Airport, turned right and started hitching. Around nightfall I got to a little town in the south-west called Queenstown, where I checked into the local youth hostel, located in what had once been a grand hotel. (It was quirky: the fire escape plan for the top floor involved a very long rope and a steel weight.) I was the only guest that night, yet the owner tucked me away up on the third floor. When I asked him why, he told me there was a major environmental stoush going on – it turned out to be the Franklin Dam dispute, which polarised the Tasmanian community that year – and that Queenstown was, in his words, a 'redneck town'. He reckoned with my long hair and beard I looked like a greenie who'd wandered into the enemy camp, and that I'd best keep out of sight.

It turned out to be good advice. When I went down to the nearby shops, nobody would talk to me. An older lady piped up: 'People like you shouldn't be allowed!' I shot back: 'Allowed what?' Man, was that the wrong thing to say. Deathly silence, everyone staring at me. I thought, 'I'm getting out of this place.' I headed back to the hotel and told the owner that I'd be leaving early next morning for Hobart. He had a warning: 'Be careful, she's a rough road.'

It was still dark when I set out hitching and there were no cars on the road. Eventually, a squad car appeared, heading back towards Queenstown. I got a big smile and wave from the cop driving.

I'd been walking several hours when I heard a car coming from behind at speed. It whipped past and came screeching to a halt, spun around in a cloud of gravel and dust and pulled up hard beside me. The driver said, 'Hop in quick, mate, we're in a hurry!' I climbed in behind two young guys, both with beer cans in hand and cigarettes hanging from their lips.

> Me: 'Thanks for picking me up, given you're in such a hurry.'
> Driver: 'Yeah, yeah, mate, we're in quite a hurry.'
> Me: 'Well, you're very kind.'
> Passenger: 'Do yah think we should tell him?'
> Driver: 'Mate, we've just stolen this car from Queenstown.'
> Me: 'Considering the circumstances, I'm awfully appreciative of you stopping for me.'

A cop car appeared coming the other way, and spun around behind us. Another soon joined and the chase was on. There was no seatbelt in the back seat so I braced myself against the door as we sped around corners. We came to a curve where a rough four-wheel-drive track forked off the highway and went flying down it.

A kilometre or so down the road we hit a stream and the car stalled in the middle. An apologetic voice came from the front seat: 'Oh, mate, so sorry we can't take you any further.' Then the pair of them took off, bolting across the river. On the other side the road branched, and they went left.

I was about to take my shoes off and climb out, when a big hairy cop arm reached through the window and grabbed me. There were about half a dozen police around the car, all armed as they are in Aussie. Hairy Arm dragged me out and slammed me against the bonnet. He was about to put the cuffs on when one of his mates – it must have been the cop who'd passed me earlier – called out: 'Leave him – that's the hitchhiker.'

The cop who'd roughed me up said, 'Mate, which way did they go?' I thought, 'Bugger you,' pointed to the right fork, and watched them all sprint off the wrong way. Then I walked back to the highway.

Later, I was picked up by a woman who told me she was looking for someone to temporarily take over her role managing the YHA at Port Arthur. I told her I'd done similar work in New Zealand, and she offered me the job. That night at the hostel I met a woman, Rosemary, who would become the mother of my daughter, my only child. Talk about forks in the road.

*

Rosemary was an artist who'd grown up in the Blue Mountains near Sydney. She was a quiet, reserved person, quite unlike me, but we had an immediate connection and quickly fell in love. It was my first romantic relationship where I felt I could share anything and everything. Like me, Rosemary loved the outdoors, and during walks together in the country around Port Arthur and later in the Blue Mountains she told me all about the flora and fauna, what berries were safe to eat and the names of the birds we heard.

Our walks were the start of another great love affair – with the Aussie bush. Something about the scent of that bush gets me. A few years ago when smoke from bushfires raging across the Tasman hung for days over Golden Bay, I had dreams in which I sat beside a campfire, the tang of eucalyptus in my nostrils. And the sounds of the Aussie bush! It's just so extraordinarily noisy, day and night. Friends and family over there who know how much I enjoy their wildlife will sometimes call me from the bush to give me a good blast of birdsong.

Comparisons are odious, they say, and when I'm walking in Australia I try to avoid measuring it against the New Zealand backcountry, but the differences are stark. And we're spoiled in New Zealand: nothing in this country bites or stings, and we can go tramping happy that we're at the top of the food chain. Across the Ditch, you always have to be hyper-aware of where you're putting your feet.

My nephew is a leading botanist and I've been out in the field with him in Australia. The forest that at first glance seems so dry and scratchy turns out to be full of botanical diversity when you examine it closely. He calls it a 'bot-fest'.

One of the longer walks I did in Australia was in the Blue Mountains. Rosemary's father 'Red' lived there. He was a one-time conscientious objector from the US who'd immigrated to Australia as a young man, and worked in conservation and on water-supply networks.

In 1980, there weren't great maps in Australia. I've since realised that New Zealand at that time had a comparatively advanced mapping system – even now the level of detail on our maps holds up well. There was only a very vague map of the Blue Mountains, but Red knew the area well, and he and his best friend, an Aboriginal elder, sketched me a route from south-west of Sydney through rough country to Katoomba, from where I planned to catch a train back to Red's place.

For the first few days everything went great. I slept under the stars – one night, I woke up to a wombat walking past.

Once, I came across a house deep in the bush that Red had marked as derelict and there turned out to be two old fellas living there who invited me in for a cup of tea. They gave me more directions, albeit pretty sketchy.

It was that day that things went pear-shaped. I was walking up a ridge, along a partly formed track, when I saw an old jersey hanging from a tree. That struck me as odd, but I continued up the ridge – or so I thought. Two hours later I found myself approaching that same jersey from the same direction. That was a very weird feeling – like vertigo, almost. I remember thinking, 'A compass would be pretty useful to have right now.' I took a step forward and there on the ground in front of me was a compass. Things like that happen in the bush and there's no use wondering why. I just yelled out 'Thanks!', got my bearings and pressed on. But it saved me from what could have been a nasty situation. I was lost in the Australian bush with no locator beacon, no way of communicating, no snake-bite kit.

Late in the afternoon, I emerged in the Katoomba River Valley, where Red's map indicated there was a tramping hut. Since he'd last been there, the building had collapsed, but I set myself up for the night beside the ruins. Just on dusk, I watched a pack of dingoes wander down the side of the river. (I've never had a problem with dingoes, but then I've never been silly enough to get too close to them. Same with snakes. If I see one of those, I keep well out of its way.) The next day I found a track among steep bluffs and climbed out of the valley to Katoomba, and from there caught the next train back to Red's.

That first trip to Australia was seminal for me. I connected with my extended family, and I met Rosemary, who followed me back to New Zealand to do some tramping in my favourite haunts. Unfortunately, it didn't work out –

she preferred living in Oz, I preferred it here. She went home, and for a while we maintained a trans-Tasman relationship, but it couldn't go on like that forever. On my last visit, I went alone to a folk festival in New South Wales and bumped into a woman, Robyn, whom I'd first met at Nambassa and subsequently hung out with at other hippie fests. Meanwhile, Rosemary had found a new man, Stephen, who's still her partner. But there was a final twist: when Rosemary and I met one last time to say goodbye, she got pregnant. I wasn't told until later, but I had a daughter.

Relax shelter, Mt Robert, Nelson Lakes National Park.

Chapter 10

After returning to New Zealand, I moved in with Robyn in the Hawke's Bay. She was training to be a Steiner School teacher, and I found work as a farmhand. As a couple we always seemed to be on unstable ground, but we did have one big idea in common: we wanted to create a cooperative community – okay, a commune. We started to tee up a few friends. We even organised a folk music festival in the Baton Valley down in Tasman to spread the word. Afterwards, a hardcore few who were interested in pursuing the vision parked up in their teepees and house trucks on a property at Tui near Motueka and began looking around for a piece of land to build something more permanent.

I wasn't among them. Robyn and I had split, and I just wanted to get away for a while. I'd scored a job managing a YHA hostel at Aoraki/Mt Cook, the perfect place to get over romantic disappointments and to lose oneself in the epic outdoors. After a week-long hostel management course with the YHA at Ōamaru, I cycled to Mt Cook Village. Soon enough I'd scored another part-time gig driving a tourist bus. I had a bus driver's licence, and I don't know how polished I was as a tour host, but my employers had told me they wanted drivers who could be their natural selves and I've never had trouble filling that brief.

Unless required for driving, I had my days free between 10 am and 5 pm. I'd head off up the Hooker Valley, or Mt Wakefield, or behind the Hermitage to Mt Kitchener, taking an ice axe and crampons with me and disappearing for most of the day, a tiny speck in the alpine landscape. I'd come back exhausted but deeply satisfied.

Every so often, I'd explore further afield. The YHA wanted me to take time away from my place of work because my accommodation was such a tiny unit, so they paid my bus trip to Timaru every two months, along with five nights in a campground cabin. Sometimes I'd head elsewhere. One of my favourite getaway places was the Lower Murchison Valley and an NZFS hut called the Liebig Hut.

Those were the days when you could walk across the surface of the Tasman Glacier – there wasn't a lake there then. You'd ford the Murchison, which was pretty straightforward, then walk upriver and through a valley to the face of the Murchison Glacier. There were two huts up there – the Liebig, which was a classic six-bunk Forest Service hut, and the Onslow/Steffan Memorial Hut. Behind the Liebig Hut there was a big saddle, and I enjoyed climbing up to explore the tops and then hurtling back down a scree slide. It was lovely to have that sense of freedom and solitude among the valleys – hardly anyone visited.

Other times, I'd go flying. I had a couple of friends who were caretakers at Unwin Hut, the alpine club's place near Mt Cook Airport. When I visited them, I'd pop over to the airport, and I'd often be offered a freebie up to the glaciers if there were unsold seats. Everyone knew I had a thing for flying.

I loved living in Mt Cook, but being enveloped by alps I'd sometimes feel hemmed in and missed the nurturing quality of the bush. I had another friend who was working at Fox Glacier, and if there was a spare seat on a scenic flight I'd hitch a ride over to Fox and spend my weekends in the West Coast rainforest, refilling my bucket.

*

After 14 months, I was keen for a change of scene. I freighted most of my gear to Blenheim, sent my bike ahead to friends in Twizel, and walked out of Mt Cook over the Copland Pass. I spent time on the West Coast, then retrieved my bike and cycled via Blenheim all the way back up the North Island to my parents' place. Along the way I got sidetracked by another New Age festival in the central North Island, and climbed Ruapehu. The festival was entertaining enough, but the climb nearly went awry when I slipped in the higher reaches of the volcano and had to self-arrest in the snow using my ice axe. I still have the scars from that mishap, and whenever I'm driving the Desert Road and spot the mountain my elbows tingle in sympathy with my younger self. After catching up with Mum and Dad, I hitched north and walked the entire length of Ninety Mile Beach to Cape Rēinga.

While tiki-touring the north I'd been in contact with Roger Frost, an old friend who was working as an instructor at Rotoiti Lodge in Nelson Lakes. Roger had latched on to a temporary employment scheme and reckoned he could set me up as an assistant instructor of outdoor education, teaching tramping, kayaking, caving, bush orientation and outdoor survival skills to kids from Nelson schools. I hopped back on my bike and was in St Arnaud within days, eager to start.

It was a terrific role. Working with the other instructors, I'd get to know all about these kids, their interests and their fears, before organising a bunch of outdoor activities that would hopefully keep most of them happy. We soon learned their biggest worry wasn't river crossings or avalanches or getting stuck in tight tunnels – it was cave wetas. The idea of being underground and coming face to face with these little insects terrified them. There was no hope of talking them out of it, so we decided the best response was to tell them a little white lie. We filled pill bottles with a dark sticky substance and told the kids it was a tried and trusted old-school weta repellent. Having smeared this stuff thickly on their faces and exposed arms, they were convinced they were now 100 per cent weta-proof and would happily enter tunnels that were just crawling with insects.

Many years later, I was in downtown Nelson when one of those Rotoiti Lodge kids, now all grown up, ran across the street to buttonhole me. He said, 'You're Paul, right, the guy who took us on those caving trips?' 'Er, yes.' 'You bastard, that was Marmite you had us spread over ourselves!'

The bonus to working at St Arnaud was that it brought me much closer to my good friends at Tui. When I got my first weekend off, I cycled down there to catch up with everyone and see how things were developing. Things were going well, as it happened. They'd found a promising piece of land at Wainui Bay, at the eastern end of Golden Bay before you head over the hill to Tōtaranui, and in time they decamped there. That shared vision was becoming a reality. For want of a better name, they called themselves the Tui Community. Initially there were around 50 people covering four generations, from babies through to seventy-somethings. They were largely self-sufficient, growing their own vegetables, selling any excess as well as arts and crafts to buy whatever they couldn't produce themselves. It was a well-balanced community in the early days, with a mix of airy-fairy hippie idealists, pragmatic types who could do what needed to be done, and a few well-financed hangers-on who weren't very practical but could contribute funding. Robyn was involved, using her Steiner training to help run home schooling for the youngest Tui kids.

Part of me wanted to sign on straight way, especially after I visited the beautiful piece of land they'd found at Wainui. But at the same time I was itching to do more solo exploring, this time overseas.

*

I went back to Australia in 1986, with the idea of working long enough to finance a bigger OE. First, though, I bought a month-long bus ticket, travelling north as far as Nambour on the Sunshine Coast, where, unbeknown to me, Rosemary, Stephen and my daughter Sequoia were living. I'd had no contact at all, although Rosemary's dad Red had kept me posted about Sequoia's milestones and sent the occasional photo.

From Nambour, I headed through the Outback to Alice Springs, down to South Australia and across the Nullarbor Plain. My ticket ran out 100 kilometres short of Perth, so I hitched the final leg into the city. In Perth I laboured on building sites, then found work at a home for young people with cerebral palsy, where I helped the staff to organise and run outdoor activities for the residents.

We organised picnics in bush clearings, barbecues on the beach, and excursions to new adventure playgrounds at Perth's public parks. The kids were amazing. I remember one girl who couldn't move but just loved to be carried into the sea and partially submerged. I don't think there's any way you could do that now, not without sign-offs in triplicate and waivers from parents, but those kids got a hell of a lot out of it.

My favourite was 14-year-old Dylan. He was in a wheelchair and had to be coaxed to say anything. When we were introduced he gave me a wry smile. 'Gidday Pete!' he said. 'No, I'm Paul.' 'How you going, Pete?' I gave up, and after that I was always Pete.

I recall one park visit with Dylan and the rest of the crew. People with cerebral palsy love to touch the ground, and Dylan was no exception. I'd taken him out of his wheelchair and he and I were sitting together among the roots of a large tree at the top of a slope. I turned my back for a second, and when I looked back Dylan had sent his wheelchair careening down the slope. I retrieved it, looked away, and he did it again. He was enjoying the sport. I thought, 'I'm going to have him on.' When he was distracted, I hastily tied his wheelchair to a root, then pretended to turn my back again to create an opportunity. Suddenly, Dylan was yelling at the top of his voice: 'Paul, you fucking bastard!' The entire group clapped and cheered. He looked annoyed, but once he realised what was happening he was okay – and he called me Paul from then on.

Brief though it was, it was one of the most enjoyable jobs I've ever had – and one of the most significant, because it taught me the importance of treating any person with dignity no matter their condition. By the time it was finished, I'd saved enough for a 'round-the-world' air ticket, starting with Canada and Alaska. My next wanderings were going to be spectacular.

Blue Range Hut, Tararua Forest Park.

Chapter 11

The passenger boats that make the run up from British Columbia to parts north are about the size of our Cook Strait Interislanders, but they navigate some dramatically narrow passages. From the head of Vancouver Island, I took a ferry to Prince Rupert, then switched to the US ferry service via Ketchikan to Haines in the northern reaches of the Alaska Panhandle. At times on the journey when we were sailing up some particularly tight channel, the forest was so close you could smell it, and more than once I spotted deer walking the water's edge.

North America was teeming with wildlife. Further north, there were caribou, moose and wolves visible from the road. That was a new experience – seeing animals further up the food chain than we are. Once on a walk north of Vancouver I heard something big moving ahead of me. I stepped over a log on a muddy section of the track and there was a giant cat footprint just starting to fill with water. On another occasion, I looked out of my tent to see a bear wandering past. It was a distance off, but still there was a feeling of vulnerability.

My plan was to hitch from Haines to Anchorage, but to join those two Alaskan dots I had to go through the Yukon, which is part of Canada. I didn't get to the border until late in the evening, after it had effectively closed to foreigners for the night. There I bumped into two equally bemused Germans, and together we decided to make camp right on the border where the survey pegs disappeared into the bush. We slept with our head in one country and our feet in the other, making a mockery of that invisible and artificial barrier.

The Yukon is described as Canada's last frontier, and it certainly felt untamed to me. Climactically, it's extreme, ranging from an average of minus 30 degrees Celsius in winter to 21-degree days in summer, and because of the effect of the Coast Range it's very dry. The flatlands are dominated by boreal forest – conifers mostly – then you're into stunted subalpine trees and tundra, and towering above it all the legendary peaks, mountains like St Elias (5489 metres) and Logan (5959) and more than a dozen others that easily top 4000 metres. The colours of the Yukon got me, too. There seemed an endless variety of greens in the lower country, then above the grassline it was all yellows, rich browns and even hints of red. Viewed on a good day, the glacier-fed lakes were stunning emeralds and turquoises – like Lake Tekapo but with the dial turned up.

At one stage I hitched a ride on a pickup truck, and my view looking back from the flatbed was of endless miles of dead-straight road. I wondered whether if you lived in that vast country you'd develop something like the thousand-mile stare of outback Australians.

I kipped at the driver's place in Anchorage, where I learned something about Alaskans' resilience in the face of nature. Originally this guy's house had been two levels, until the top floor was ripped off by a hurricane. He'd responded not by shifting out, but by sealing off the top with a rubbery membrane and moving everything downstairs. Apparently quite a few locals had done it!

He took me for a quick tour of Anchorage, which was another eye-opener. In the city's outskirts, I witnessed an airplane taking off on a back street, and saw other planes parked up on people's front lawns. This was exciting. I'd read about the Alaskan experience of aviation, how the early bush pilots had picked up where the explorers left off, landing on the same iced-up rivers once used by dog-sledders, or hopping from lake to lake on floats. The airplane was the perfect vehicle for Alaska, not only because of its vastness, but also the extremes of climate that make road infrastructure so marginal. A lot of the state is in permafrost, and when temperatures rise the land can shift dramatically. For trappers, miners and anyone else wanting to access the hinterland, flying ruled. In the winter, they put skis on the planes, and in summer floats or wheels.

It's still like that. I've heard that one in four Alaskans owns a plane, and that makes sense to me – they're far more convenient than road transport in many cases and can be cheap to run if well tuned. Piper Cubs and two-seater Cessnas are common, and you see a few locally developed aircraft like the little Arctic Tern bush plane. They're all modified with high-powered engines so you can make short landings and takeoffs, with fat tyres for the tundra and removable seats so they can be stuffed with provisions and gear. In Anchorage, people keep a plane like we would a 4WD, to access their cabins in the hills or to go fishing or hunting. They just roll it out onto the road and go – and motorists must always give way. I even heard that the national parks use bush planes to pick up rubbish from the tundra!

The Alaskan people were remarkable in all sorts of ways. In a little place called Tok Junction, I unwittingly set off a diner full of locals when I started eating flapjacks without adding the customary condiment. The guy who served me told me, 'Put some syrup on those, man!' Maple syrup's a luxury at home and so I just drizzled on a little. When I looked up, everyone in the diner was staring. The bloke whispered, 'They're watching you, man, keep putting it on until I say stop.' I started hosing it over my plate and slowly people went back to their business.

I was still working on those pancakes when there was a sudden engine roar. Outside, a de Havilland Otter was taxiing up the main street. It disgorged seven or eight people, plus dogs, and they all walked over for breakfast. I got talking to the pilot, an Inuit guy, who told me he'd been flying planes for nearly 50 years. I asked, 'Where did you learn to fly?' He looked at me: 'Learn to fly? No, I'm an eagle. Only white men need to learn how to fly.'

It was an apt comment, given where I was heading. From Tok Junction, I planned to hitch my way out of Alaska as far south as Oshkosh, Wisconsin, in time for the opening weekend of the world's largest aviation event, the EAA AirVenture. This week-long celebration of flight was something I badly wanted to experience, which is why I'd left myself a full week to get there. But maybe I'd miscalculated? Standing on the highway with my thumb out, I was approached by a local who cheerfully informed me I had no show of hitching out of Tok Junction, and that a similarly deluded Frenchman had just given up after five days trying.

Perhaps it was my honest Kiwi face – or sudden desperation – but I wasn't there long before a driver pulled up. Rolling down his window, he asked where I was heading. Just to be a smart arse, I said 'Oshkosh!' It was the truth, but Oshkosh was also more than 5000 kilometres away.

He shot back: 'You mean Wisconsin?'

'Well, actually, yes.'

'I live just north of Oshkosh. Hop in.'

Pete was a park ranger, heading home after a season in Alaska, and he knew all the best scenic spots. We'd stop somewhere and walk for a couple of hours to some incredible landscape. It was a brilliant five-day trip, crossing through North Montana and North Dakota, camping at night or staying with friends of his en route. He finally dropped me off just short of Minneapolis.

In downtown Minneapolis, I asked a woman for directions to the nearest information centre. She said it would be closed for the day, then asked what I was up to in town. When I told her, she got excited. 'Oshkosh? Oh you have to meet my uncle! He's flying his airplane over there this week!'

It turned out that her uncle Joe owned a vintage Republic Seabee, an amphibious airplane that dates back to the 1940s. He had work to do on it before the airshow and when I told him I was a former aircraft mechanic, he pressed me into service. We fabricated a piece of cowling around the engine and did various bits and pieces, and when it was all approved, we flew to Oshkosh with his cousin and his cousin's son on board.

One thing about the US that I've never quite got to grips with is the scale at which everything happens. On that 1987 visit to Oshkosh – the first of four I've made over the years – there were close to 27,000 aircraft!

(Years later on a trip to Yosemite National Park, I would be taken aback by the size of the crowds. Welcome to the great American wilderness! Thankfully, all the human craziness was channelled into a handful of iconic landmarks such as Glacier Point, which I gave a wide berth. The

Oshkosh event has only got bigger since then. At last count, it drew a million people over the course of a week, with 100,000 camping out at the venue.)

I'd been reading about Oshkosh for years, but what I hadn't realised was the camaraderie involved. You feel like you're part of a family of aviation nuts. And when people found out I was from New Zealand, they were incredibly welcoming. One morning, the vintage airplane club were staging what they called a 'flyout breakfast' to Shawano, a plane-friendly town 100-odd kilometres away. I wandered in to the briefing and heard someone saying they were looking for a passenger. Well, my hand shot up quicker than you could say 'Oshkosh'. I flew up there in one vintage aircraft, enjoyed a delicious breakfast paid for by some anonymous benefactor in the group, then flew back in a different classic plane.

More than anything, Oshkosh was a captivating reminder of the sheer variety of aircraft. There were thousands of vintage planes, many of them immaculately restored; homebuilt microlights of every description; decommissioned airliners; and scores of military machines dating back to the First World War. The oldest airplane I've ever seen flying was a 1914 Bleriot at Oshkosh. On a later visit to the event, I flew in a 1923 Ford Trimotor with the most beautiful Art Deco interior. I stepped out of that, walked to the other end of the airfield and boarded a Concorde, which had flown from England to do four domestic joy-flights. The $US765 for an hour's flight was possibly the best money I've ever spent. Following that, I visited the microlight area and went for a ride in what was essentially a two-seat powered parachute! As a former aircraft mechanic, I found those extremes of technology on display at Oshkosh fascinating.

When it was all over, someone offered me a flight to Indianapolis in their Cessna 172. From there I hitched to St Louis, Missouri, to catch up with friends, then recommenced my globetrotting. Next stop, London.

Mangamingi Stream Hut, Hawke's Bay.

Chapter 12

I'd always felt drawn to the UK. As I mentioned, my father was born on Jersey Island, and my mother's stories of living in London before and during the war had always intrigued me. In practical terms, too, it was appealing: I've got a British passport because of Dad, and that meant I could work my away around England and Scotland for a year. I managed a couple of YHAs, worked in a printing factory near London and did a bit of WWOOFing in Wales, and in my spare time I walked.

There's a strong culture of what they call 'rambling' in the UK. Some farm owners had put up signs that said 'We welcome caring ramblers', and village pubs and tearooms were often set up to cater for walkers. One afternoon I arrived in heavy rain at a tiny village called Brasington – Mum's family name! – that had a pub, three or four houses and a tearooms. I entered the pub dripping wet, and the barman gave me a rousing welcome: 'Put your wet gear there, son, and pull up a seat by the fire!'

Mostly I stayed at YHA hostels, which tend to be strategically placed along the rambling routes. They're often in the hills, usually at the back of a farm, and can look a bit like one of our Kiwi backcountry huts, with a communal dining area and one or two bunkrooms. They're basic but they have everything you need. As a result, a lot of hikers travel very light. A friend of mine walked all the way from Land's End in south-west England to John o' Groats in north-eastern Scotland without a sleeping bag, staying at hostels and B & Bs.

Unfortunately, given that this was the UK, it was always likely that you'd be caught out by the weather. I remember arriving at a remote lake in the Scottish Highlands when it suddenly started hailing violently. Luckily, there was a wee stone bothy nearby to take shelter in. A bothy, for those who don't know, is an old stone hut that is open for anyone to use. They're often small and basic, with just a fireplace, and can be centuries old. Wherever I walked in the UK, I savoured that sense of the deep past. I'd be walking and come upon a stone wall that had been there for 1000 years, or an ancient battle site or a 400-year-old farmhouse.

(Not that tramping in New Zealand lacks a sense of history. During long walks through Te Urewera I've found midden evidence of people camping there centuries ago, and the Whanganui River area is reliably fascinating. My friend the late Jim Larsen had an air service at Tākaka and I'd regularly fly with him to the head of the Waitōtara Valley in Taranaki, where his family had a farm, then disappear for a week into the heavy bush between Taranaki and Whanganui. Once I followed the Matemateāonga Track, an old Māori trail and a settler dray road that ends at the Whanganui; on other trips I spied signs of early, doomed, attempts to farm – they all ended with the forest winning. In the South Island, too, I've stumbled on remote backcountry homestead sites, old fencelines or pack tracks. And of course in Otago and on the West Coast there are all the historic goldmining and scheelite mining sites. I'm constantly amazed at where people were willing to live and what they were prepared to endure to stake a claim.)

In Wales, I did a three-day coastal walk. I did another three-dayer in the Peaks District and the same again in the Lakes District, both in England. I did long walks, too, in the Scottish Highlands, a place that really got under my skin. Even though you're never far from civilisation as the crow flies, there's still a strong feeling of being in the back of beyond when you're walking in the Highlands. You leave a farm, cross over a ridge and you might as well be at the head of the Rangitātā River.

Beyond the Highlands, I was struck by the proximity of public walking routes to private lives. In Britain, you can be walking through farmland on a public laneway and next moment you're passing right beside the farmer's old stone cottage. Or you're in a national park, yet there are villages along the way serving bangers and mash and foaming pints. Imagine finding a tearooms beside the Travis Hut! I was pleasantly surprised, too, by the diversity of landscape, from peaks to lowland grasslands to river valleys to open tops and old-growth forest.

As for the walking tracks themselves, generally they weren't as well formed as in New Zealand, but the maps in the UK were brilliant, so detailed that they'd even show rock markers and often with helpful written descriptions. Certainly you didn't need to scan for triangles of coloured tin hammered into tree trunks.

I walked through some spooky landscapes, particularly in the Scottish Highlands. It's something I tend to pick up on wherever I go – 'I don't want to hang around here!' It's not something you can put into words, just an eerie feeling about a place. Once I was walking along some alpine tops in New Zealand and had an unnerving feeling that something was 'off'. Soon after, I came across a piece of aluminium on the ground that had clearly been part of a plane – I was at the site of a fatal aeroplane crash. On another trip, I walked along a ridge that gave off a similarly unsettling vibe. When I described the experience to a friend who'd mustered sheep in the area, he told me about finding a film canister at the same spot. When developed, it turned out to be the final photos taken by a solo climber who'd fallen to his death there years earlier.

*

Shortly before I arrived on Jersey Island, a massive storm tore through Britain. I was staying in Essex at the time, and we'd woken to Saharan dust sandblasting the streets, while other areas around the UK were briefly without power. On Jersey, some massive old oak trees had been uprooted and glasshouses flattened, among the general devastation.

I wasn't sure what to expect of Jersey. It's not much bigger than Waiheke Island, but has ten times the population, so it's quite built up, particularly the main centre, St Helier. About half the island is cultivated, with less than a quarter left over for the natural environment. But what an environment! The coastline switches between soaring cliffs, wide bays and golden-sanded beaches. As a young girl, my grandmother had enjoyed one beach in particular, regularly walking along it, around a headland and through the adjacent valley. I located some of her old haunts, and it really did feel like I was walking in her footsteps.

From the town fringe, it was only a few minutes' walking before you were into bucolic countryside, all meadowland, wild flowers and hedgerows. The farms were generally small and, as in mainland Britain, the public lanes ran close beside farmhouses. I became very fond of the island's historic stone walls, which were supplemented by dense hedges of barberry and hawthorn. In places, the vegetation emerged from the top of the walls and was nested in by robins, sparrows and other birds. I wandered everywhere, following old paths down gullies and streams, through woodland, stopping to take in the valley views.

On my second day on Jersey, I tracked down the house where Dad had spent the first three years of his life. The woman who answered the door was intrigued by my story – her people, she told me, were French-speaking Jersey Islanders just like my grandmother. The parallels continued: my ancestors had owned a bakery across the road; her family now owned and operated a café out of the same building. Eventually, her father joined us, and told me that the house and bakery/café had always been owned by French-speaking Jersey Islanders. Before I left, I took photos of the house. When I showed them to Dad months later, he recognised everything, but only as high up as the windowsill – he'd been a toddler there, after all.

I visited Guernsey Island as well and was keen to explore further, but my round-the-world ticket was about to expire. Sadly, after just a few days on the islands, I had to go. I left with a far more vivid sense of what my father's family had left behind when they sailed for New Zealand, but no answers to some big questions. Biggest of all: why did they leave? Clearly, they saw an opportunity on the other side of the world, but was that the only reason for such a profound uprooting? They didn't tell their families that they weren't coming back – perhaps because they hadn't yet made that mental shift. My grandmother had several sisters who stayed behind on Jersey. Their letters suggest that on both sides there was an expectation that one day Dad's family would return to the island, but they never did.

My ticket took me back via Sydney, and I went straight from the airport to the Blue Mountains. I'd been awake for 24 hours when I arrived at Red's place, but he'd laid on a surprise – an Aboriginal meditation bush camp at the western end of the mountains, where he'd arranged a tent for me to sleep off my jet lag. I crawled into my sleeping bag at 2.30 pm and didn't stir until lunchtime the following day, when I woke to the sounds of the Aussie bush in all its glory. It was the deepest sleep I think that I've ever had, but I needed it for what was coming next.

While overseas I'd had a letter from Rosemary and Stephen inviting me to meet Sequoia. There was a condition, however: I couldn't tell her that I was her dad.

I caught an inter-state bus to Brisbane, then another bus north to the village of Mapleton, near Nambour, inland Sunshine Coast Region. I was incredibly nervous when Stephen met me at the bus station. I'd never met him before, but he immediately put me at ease with a warm greeting and a hug.

Sequoia was five, home schooled, a bright and imaginative kid, and the spitting image of my mother at that age. The family lived in the bush, and she started off by showing me the special places in the forest where her imaginary friends lived, then described for me what the birds were saying. I saw that she had incredible bush sense for a young kid. She knew which plants were edible and which ones you had to avoid, and she took her role of educating me very seriously.

I stayed with them for two weeks, abiding by Rosemary and Stephen's wishes. But it wasn't always easy. I kept looking at her, thinking, 'What an amazing child', and 'This wonderful person is my daughter!' It was overwhelming at times. I found myself wishing that things had been different.

Interestingly, after I got back to New Zealand, Sequoia told Rosemary, 'You know that nice man Paul who stayed here? I feel like I've known him from before I was born.' That moved us both to tears.

Sequoia didn't learn the truth about me until she was 11. Then she wrote me a letter. It began 'Dear Dad', which I found so moving. From then on we wrote a lot of letters – I still have boxes and boxes of hers – and I flew to Australia regularly to see her. Unfortunately, it got messy for Rosemary and particularly for Stephen, even though it had been his idea for me to meet Sequoia. She felt hurt that it had taken them so long to tell her the truth. In the end, I helped to mend fences and for the last few years things between all of us have been great.

*

When I got back to New Zealand, I had a lot to ponder. I still hadn't fully digested what I'd seen in North America and Europe, from hitching through the vastness of the Yukon to riding the packed London Underground, but I had a deepening awareness of social, political and environmental realities that I hadn't previously contemplated in any depth. And then there were the emotions stirred up by meeting Sequoia. My first thought when I landed in Auckland was that I needed to disappear into the quiet mountains for a while.

Tunnel Creek Hut, Paringa River.

Chapter 13

Two weeks later I was in deepest Fiordland, working as a temporary hut warden on the Milford Track. Some old friends in Te Anau, Bill and Adele, needed help with the annual post-season track and hut clean-up, and I stumbled into the job. With winter not far off, the first priority was to remove all of the footbridges above the bushline that might be at risk from avalanche, and then we got stuck in to cleaning the huts. There was so much rubbish; we filled dozens of wool-bale sacks with the stuff people left behind. On my days off, I walked the track from one end to the other, revelling in having this piece of Fiordland all to myself.

When the work was finished, I said goodbye to Bill and Adele and went looking for new country in Mt Aspiring National Park. I headed up Camerons Creek, which flows into the Makarora, then over the tops to the head of the Hunter Valley. Ahead, the land rose sharply to a steep ice- and snow-covered mountainside, beyond which lay the Wills Saddle. It looked a little tricky but I had an ice axe and was confident. Halfway up, however, I was starting to wonder. I was inching my way up a chimney-like gap between two faces, one of ice and one of rock, using all the strength in my arms and legs to keep moving upwards. But where the hell was I going? Above me was a cornice. I wedged myself as securely as possible to cut through the overhanging snow and ice. I was awkwardly positioned, my muscles ached and my hands were cold and I couldn't see whether I was making any progress, but I kept at it until finally I broke through. Using the axe as an anchor, I hauled myself onto the top of the bluff, crawled to solid ground and lay there exhausted.

I heard footsteps. Was I dreaming? I looked up and there was a great bull tahr. From the ground it looked bloody huge, and it was moving my way. Clearly it hadn't sensed me. I gripped my ice axe, caught between fear and wishing I had a camera. It was only a couple of metres away when it froze, sniffed the air, and leaped off the bluff. I was stunned. It must have plummeted dozens of metres to a thin ledge below, but instead of stopping it compressed itself and sprang to another ledge further down, and so on. Within seconds, the animal was on the valley floor where I'd begun my hours-long ascent.

After my David Attenborough moment, I worked my way down into the Wills Valley. It was hard going, with a worrying amount of avalanche debris in the gullies. The Wills River was raging with snow melt, but I made it through without incident to tussock country, and finally there was Wills Hut. I anticipated spending extra time there given how high the river was running, and as it happened I was marooned for three nights. I knew people would start to worry that I hadn't made it out, but I wasn't going to attempt that crossing until the water dropped.

Eventually I made it out to the Gates of Haast, and hitched through to the Coast. In South Westland, I ventured up to the head of the Paringa River, where I experienced a repeat performance of my marooning at Wills Hut. In this case, however, the Paringa was uncrossable due not to snow melt, but a biblical rain.

Stuck, I lit a fire, gave the hut a good scrub, then looked around for something to keep boredom at bay. On a high shelf, I spotted a very old transistor radio. I fiddled with the dial, and in came music. National Radio! Weirdly, though, the news bulletins were two hours late. Finally, I twigged: it was Australian national radio. That's how, in a rain-lashed West Coast backcountry hut, I got the news that the region was dealing with a once-in-600-year weather event. The Aussies told me!

While I twiddled my thumbs, I counted my blessings. I was in the New Zealand backcountry, my second home. I thought, 'This is what I've come back for!' I felt enriched by my experiences overseas, and more accepting of aspects of my past. 'It is what it is,' I thought, 'and it is part of who I am now.'

That also went for Robyn and the Tui Community. After our break-up, I'd discounted being part of that joint project. But while in the UK, I'd received letters from other friends at Tui prodding me to get involved. Waiting out the storm, I turned it over in my mind.

When I finally came out of the Paringa Valley it was still raining like mad, but I soon hitched a lift. Coincidentally, the driver was heading to Golden Bay, so I tagged along. That night in the Bay, I stayed with some old friends, and they mentioned they were sailing to Wainui Bay the following morning for a picnic with the Tui people. Did I want to come? Clearly, someone upstairs was trying to tell me something! I needed to go to Tui and see how it felt. I went for the day and ended up staying for 11 years.

Baikie Hut, Twizel River.

Chapter 14

Locals branded Tui 'the German commune', but that wasn't accurate. Of the 40 or so pioneers, only four were from Germany and the rest came from all over. I was impressed with what they'd achieved. There were a lot of practical, experienced and knowledgeable people, including a retired building engineer and a practising draughtsman, and Tui had a reputation for getting things done. When it came to building houses, you'd draw up a plan and the local building inspector would ask, 'Has Rheinhard had a look at this? What about Frank? Well if they're happy with it that's a good start.'

Even so, the council remained very nervous about any unorthodox use of land. Multiple occupancy particularly challenged them, and they imposed endless conditions. Interestingly, the most sympathetic voices in our corner were from neighbouring farmers. At the public hearing, after all the objections to our application for multiple occupancy were read out – most from holidaymakers who spent two weeks a year in the Bay – one of these farmers stood up. He said words to the effect of 'How dare you abuse these people? They might be hippies, but they're my neighbours, and they're finally doing something positive with that piece of land!'

How did Tui operate? First you had to become a member, and that depended largely on your ability to get along with others. Once you were in, you'd have a parcel of land on which to build your low-cost housing, and everyone pitched in to help. I put together plans for a tiny house, had it approved by the council and assembled some building materials, but then decided against it. Instead, I lived in a caravan up the slope with a big roof over the top and a composting toilet in the bush nearby. (I gave that caravan away when I left; it's gone now and the roof is currently being used as someone's shed.) We had a massive vege garden to supply all our needs, and sold the excess. Later, we established small businesses.

I was the coordinator for one enterprise, a skincare range called Tui Balms that used organic beeswax and olive oils scented with sandalwood. We started off with a small run of 100-gram jars of bee balm, selling mainly through health-food stores. When it took off, the range was expanded to include lip balms, insect repellents and massage waxes. Soon, what had started as a cottage industry became a busy commercial operation. We shifted manufacturing from the back of the laundry to a dedicated facility with a full commercial kitchen.

On Friday afternoons I'd check the hundreds of orders that had come in during the week, and then I'd start manufacturing. Night-time was best because the smell was intense, although the downside was that I struggled to sleep afterwards. On Saturday and Sunday I'd pack the orders, and on Monday morning I'd take all the packages on my motorbike to the Tākaka courier office.

I was also put in charge of Tui's sewage utilisation scheme. The council had insisted we take care of our sewage ourselves, so we designed what they call a 'tree field utilisation scheme'. We set up pipelines from every house to a settling pond and when the level got high I'd turn on a pump and send it across to a ten-acre block of trees that I'd planted. The grass between the trees would be harvested once a month using an old tractor and made into compost.

I got regular soil samples taken. We were apparently one hundred times purer than the allowable level for a city park, so clearly our scheme worked pretty well. They've since changed the system, and that field of trees is now the Tui Events Centre where they hold personal growth workshops and other events. It's such a pleasant area these days you'd have no idea what it was once used for!

Meanwhile, I'd also taken on a job for DOC repairing track signs for the section of the Abel Tasman between Wainui and Awaroa. Sometimes I'd base myself at the Tui Community barn, which was a good spot to repaint signs on wet days, but I had another stack of signs at Whariwharangi Hut and a third lot at DOC's Tōtaranui workshop. I'd alternate between the three, interspersed with the odd bit of hut warden work. DOC gave me a motorbike, but I was super fit and liked to walk or run as much as possible. I'd run over the Gibbs Hill track between Wainui and Tōtaranui, knocking off what would be a four-hour walk in just over an hour.

I wasn't alone in being so busy. At Tui, there were constant working bees, from vege gardening, to planting trees in the orchard and shelter belts, to building visitor accommodation. A gong would sound and people would turn up. That changed as more people joined the community. Cooperative communities always attract dreamers as well as doers, and we had our fair share of impractical types, but early on there was a nice balance. There will always be personal conflicts, too, but we had pretty good communication. Some people got bored with the constant meetings, but those exchanges nipped a lot of potential conflicts in the bud.

I felt at home at Tui – mostly. The wandering part of me, the Paul Kilgour who lived for a stormy night in a remote backcountry hut, wasn't entirely placated.

Eric Biv, also known as Agony Island Biv, in the Havelock River valley, Canterbury.

Chapter 15

In the winter of 1989 I received a tempting offer. Four friends from Golden Bay were keen for me to join them on a sea-kayaking odyssey around D'Urville Island in the Marlborough Sounds. The instigator was my great mate (the now late) Gavin Cederman, who'd also roped in both his current and former girlfriends and one of their male cousins. We took a double and three single kayaks and went for two weeks.

I'd never done much kayaking, but soon learned the ins and outs, as well as all about currents and tides, and how, when you have a tide race, you always head seawards for safety, even when you're cold and wet and that's the last thing you want to do.

The highlight of the fortnight was a visit to predator-free Stephens Island. It's best known as a sanctuary for tuatara, but it's also home to rare species of gecko, the endemic Hamilton's Frog and an enormous number of seabirds, and it's just a fantastically wild place. A friend had arranged permission for us to stay on the island, and the DOC caretaker, John Mitchell, was expecting us.

As we paddled across from D'Urville Island, I sighted John bounding from rock to rock like a mountain goat, yelling out instructions on where to land. We hid the kayaks away in a dip behind some rocks way above the high-tide mark. We didn't realise it was where the seals slept, so our kayaks stunk of seal for months after that trip, despite some vigorous scrubbing.

We spent three nights on Stephens Island, before kayaking to the middle of the Rangitoto Islands, home for almost 50 years to the legendary Ross Weber. John gave us some mail and a batch of home brew for Ross and we paddled off with a massive storm building behind us.

The D'Urville Island trip gave me a real bug for kayaking, which I found complemented tramping by working my upper body and allowed me to get into places that were tricky to reach on foot. Gavin became my regular kayaking buddy. He lived near the Motupipi River and could easily drag his kayak down the grass into the river and start paddling, and I kept mine beside the water at the Tui Community. We did several trips around the Abel Tasman National Park coastline, from headland to headland. Once we even paddled from Golden Bay to a dentist's appointment in Nelson. We kayaked as far as we could up the Maitai River, stashed our kayaks and walked through town to my dentist's offices.

Gavin was also involved in my other big sea-kayaking adventure to date, a fortnight exploring the southern reaches of Stewart Island with him, *New Zealand Geographic*'s Kennedy Warne and Carl Walrond and his brother. Some hunters agreed to boat us and our kayaks in to Port Pegasus, and we spent the next two weeks exploring various arms and bays, climbing up rocky outcrops and walking through the hills. We ventured deep into the Tin Range, so named because in the 1880s it was the site of a tin-mining 'rush' after tin ore was discovered. It's fascinating country, with mining relics and tramlines secreted away in the bush.

I enjoyed kayaking, but it didn't entirely scratch my itch for adventure. Back at Tui, I still yearned for the backcountry, to go deep into the bush on my own.

One night, I couldn't sleep. Next to my bed was a bunch of old inch-to-the mile maps. I grabbed one at random – the Whitcombe River Valley, near Hokitika. By the end of the week I was on my way to the West Coast.

My plan was a one-man trek across the Main Divide and down into the gravel plains of the Rakaia Valley. I'd be roughly following, albeit in reverse, some of the route taken by Jakob Lauper and John Whitcombe in autumn 1863, when they endured two weeks of storms and perilous river crossings searching for a way through for a road connection between Canterbury and the West Coast.

Whitcombe, a young surveyor, and Lauper, a Swiss-born alpine guide turned goldminer, had a brutal time. Accounts tend to use phrases like 'epic hardship' and 'extreme deprivation'. They set out from the Canterbury side woefully under-provisioned and with no tent. The country turned out to be far more challenging than they anticipated, all steep-sided gorges, exposed ridges and chokingly dense West Coast rainforest. Hit by persistent downpours and occasional snow, they managed perhaps five kilometres a day, sleeping when they could on hard, sodden ground, their biscuits and some other provisions pulped by the rain. By the time they reached the coast, they were emaciated and desperate. It ended tragically, with Whitcombe drowning while attempting to cross the Taramakau River in search of a Māori village and food.

It's one of those pioneering stories that underscore just how dangerous crossing the Main Divide can be. Of course, in my case I had maps, a modern pack and tramping clothes and equipment, and a known route to follow. I was also far better provisioned, with enough dehydrated meals and high-energy bars to keep me going for weeks on end. But I wasn't expecting it to be easy. It was July, the middle of a raw winter, and at times I'd find that my feet were actually warmer fording an icy mountain river than walking through the deep snow piled either side. And while I yearned to be alone in the wilderness, I'd never previously gone so far solo.

But one thing I did 'lack' was a sense of time. A cheap watch I'd bought from a petrol station on the Coast crapped out on day two. I threw it on the fire, and the next morning not a single part of it could be found among the ashes. I took it as a sign: time wasn't going to be my master. I'd wake up and think, 'I feel like walking', and get cracking. I'd stop only when I felt hungry. Sometimes more than half a day would pass before I'd feel the need to eat something. I got away with two meals a day, and felt strong. On a couple of occasions I woke up ready to roll, and charged out of the hut to find it was still pitch black. It was on this trip that I came up with my tramping motto, 'One step at a time is really good walking.' Instead of being focused on your destination or making good time, you have to make sure to enjoy the moment.

I started out from the Taipo River, inland from Kumara Junction on the western side of Arthur's Pass, then wound my way south, to the Arahura River, then on to Grassy Flat and the Mungo River, a tributary of the Hokitika. It had been raining steadily before I reached Poet Hut, so I decided to take a rest day.

The hut was a 1960s four-bunker, with a decent fireplace but a roof that had seen better days. I sited my billy to catch the worst of the leaks, and that rainwater proved handy when the rivers turned muddy and undrinkable over the following days. Immediately behind, the terrain rose steeply and was heavily forested. More than once I contemplated what would be left of me if the heavy rain unleashed a tree avalanche. In front lay the roiling Mungo River.

That afternoon I was watching the river rising when I heard a huge rumble that shook the hut. Something massive – probably a very large boulder – had shifted in the rushing waters. Two days later, after the rain had cleared and the river dropped to a safe level, I crossed, then climbed over Frew Saddle and down Frew Creek.

The pass named for John Whitcombe is one of the lowest on the Main Divide. From the West Coast side, you walk for three days up the Whitcombe Valley, rising slowly out of the valley and into the bushline, until suddenly you find you're up on Whitcombe Pass. It wasn't a dramatic climb at all. Crossing it was a different matter. It was murky weather, low cloud, and I practically had to swim through deep spindrift then take care on the other side to avoid slipping into Louper Stream (the waterway was misnamed after Jakob Lauper).

Perversely, it was then that I had the bright idea of extending my walk. My body and mind were feeling good – I was travelling through new country, which is always a buzz for me – and I had enough food for at least a couple more weeks. Why not just keep going, and see how far I could push it?

I recently read a book by a well-travelled Kiwi backcountry walker, George Spearing. George once walked from Land's End to John o' Groats in the UK, and then knocked off Mexico to Canada. He also cycled across the Nullarbor from Kalgoorie to Port Australia. George reckons he never knew quite how to respond when people asked him why he walked these massive distances. If they had to ask, he reckoned, they wouldn't understand the answer. Because the truth is that every day when you're in that mode you have a goal in front of you and a sense of achievement when you reach it, plus you're in amazing country where it means something to be alive. George is in his eighties now, and living in Southland. I wrote to him recently to say that what he wrote absolutely chimed with my experience.

So, I was going to spend another week or two in the mountains. But how could I let my safety person – in this case, my friend Neil at Tui – know my revised plan? Neil knew my abilities and wouldn't panic easily, but if I didn't show within a few days of my designated finish date he'd have to call the authorities. Luckily, a few hours from the road-end of the Rakaia Valley I bumped into a farmer out mustering. I said, 'Mate, I've got to get a message out to a guy to let him know that I'm safe and well but planning to walk on.' He told me I was welcome to head down to the homestead and make a phone call. When I added that I had a bunch of mail to post – I tend to write a lot of letters when I'm walking – he said to leave them on the kitchen table and he'd make sure they were sent out. New Zealand backcountry hospitality strikes again.

My new plan was to explore some of the big valleys on the eastern side of the Main Divide. I was going to follow my nose up the Mathias Valley, through Mt Algidus Station, up the Wilberforce River, then over a pass into the Craigieburn Forest Park. On the way I stayed in a tiny A-frame hut on the Bealey Saddle that was almost completely covered in snow. As soon as I put my pack down, I got to work on a fire, and stoked it at regular intervals through the evening. Man, was it cold up there!

It had been a lonely adventure, in the sense that for 26 days I saw no one other than that musterer in the Rakaia Valley and a solitary helicopter, which hovered overhead at Grassy Flat, then flew off when I gave them a thumbs up. On my penultimate day, however, I was approaching a hut when I caught a whiff of something cooking. It turned out to be a barbecue to celebrate the end of a police search-and-rescue training weekend, and the guys invited me to stop for a feed. After 27 days of tramping rations, that barbecue dinner tasted unbelievably good.

I came out to Highway 73 at Bealey Bridge the following day, tired but deeply satisfied. I'd come through vast and quite remarkable country, most of it new to me. I'd skirted some potentially risky situations, dipped my toe into danger, but hadn't felt out of my depth. And I'd had time alone with my thoughts. I returned to Tui feeling like I'd got something out of my system — for a while, at least — and that I could settle back happily into community life. And so I did, until an accident upended everything.

It was a lunchtime — we still had communal lunches then — when the phone rang down the passageway. I took the call and ran to the lunch place to deliver the message. The dining room was a step lower, and as I leaped I whacked my head on the top of the door and split my skull open. I saw a silver flash turning to black and went out cold, the back of my head hitting the concrete doorstep. Apparently I sat up and said, 'Now that I have your attention, there's a phone message for Cathy', then went out again. A guy carried me to a car, and drove me to Nelson Hospital.

Thus began a long, slow process of sorting myself out. Initially after being knocked out, when I opened my eyes everyone seemed to have huge bodies that tapered away to tiny heads. There was a distortion going on, and it continued. I found that I struggled to walk up the hill to my caravan. It felt like I was falling into the hill, and when I walked down I felt I was keeling backwards. In the end, someone loaned me a house-truck near the community house. A Mexican-American woman who was WWOOFing at Tui gave me regular head massages, which really helped. There were so many caring people, so much kindness.

But the accident had a legacy. Ever since, I've had trouble learning new things; I can get overwhelmed; I struggle with digital technology more than perhaps I might. Memory can be an issue, too – although I seem to have no trouble recalling in vivid detail the backcountry huts I've visited and trips I've made.

People said there was a character change in me, too. It's hard to know when you're in your own head, of course, but emotionally I do seem to be triggered more easily. Recently, a group of us did a long day walk up the Rob Roy Track off the Matukituki Valley, and as we got into the beech forest I burst into tears. I love beech forest! So it's that kind of thing. The people who know me don't judge; they think it's cool that I can be my unfiltered self.

St Winifred Hut, Havelock River.

Chapter 16

In the mid-1990s, I signed up as a full-time DOC hut warden and worker on the Heaphy Track. The work got me into the bush, obviously, but the bit I enjoyed more than I expected was the PR aspect: meeting trampers, talking about the track and collecting fees for the four huts at the Golden Bay end. This was before the booking system was introduced, but there was still an expectation that people would 'pay for their stay', and it was the job of the hut wardens to rattle the collecting dish. I proved pretty good at it, and for a while held the record for the most money collected in hut fees in a two-week period. I went in with a $50 float and came out with $800. None of it was from pressuring people to buy tickets; I just yarned with them, and shared my enthusiasm.

Not that it was all plain sailing. Near Brown Hut, I'd bumped into a group of trampers. One of them, a guy from Belgium, had gotten very irate, saying, 'I'm not paying any damn hut fee!' and punching me in the stomach – or trying to: he hit the money bag, never realising he'd just smacked 800 dollars in cash, before roaring off down the track. They nabbed him days later on the West Coast.

Prior to the North-west Nelson Forest Park becoming Kahurangi National Park, a lot of mountain bikers were convinced they wouldn't be allowed onto the Heaphy again, so there was a mad rush to bike it while they still could as there were no rules saying they could not cycle it. I took a photo of Saxon Hut with 60 bikes parked around it; earlier that day I'd seen at least 100 passing through. I worked on the first day of official mountain bike trials on the Heaphy Track and welcomed the first riders.

Partway through the year I got shoulder-tapped to be trained for DOC helicopter work. There was always plenty of that – taking out rubbish from the huts, bringing in track workers, supplies and equipment to build and repair track infrastructure. One of my jobs was to build footbridges, and all the timber and other materials had to be flown in. I remember we built the buttresses for a bridge at Blue Duck Creek, then, over the radio, described to the Tākaka workshop precisely how to shape the end of the poles for the base. When the chopper eventually lowered them into place, they fitted perfectly.

Most of my flying was with Nelson-based pilot Bill Reid. Bill was a fantastic pilot to be paired with, and a great guy. When he delivered firewood to the Heaphy huts, he would swing the net to get it as close as possible to the woodsheds. At Gouland Downs Hut he practically swung it inside! At that point, most pilots would unhook and fly off for the next lot; Bill landed in the tussocks and helped me stack the wood.

There were other moments flying with Bill that showcased his skill. For instance, we had a regular route over the northern end of the Brown River, around Mt Perry and down to the Perry Saddle Hut. Helicopter controls are super sensitive – it's all about fine adjustments. Yet on that particular route, Bill's movements were often quite dynamic. I realised that he was sensing the turbulence, reading the bush below and responding in a way that kept the chopper flying smoothly. Like a lot of good pilots, he was beautifully tuned in to his surroundings.

The privately owned Paringa/Ōtoko Junction Hut, 2020.

Chapter 17

In 1996, my father, Bob, died. I wasn't close to my father until about three years before his death. He and my mother never got over me leaving the air force to become what Dad called a 'hitchhiking bum'. And then I end up living on a commune for 11 years! But in 1993 he came to stay with me at the Tui Community for a few weeks and something between us shifted – like that rock in the Mungo River. Finally, he 'got' me.

Dad constantly surprised me on that visit. He'd mellowed since my mother's death a few years earlier. Caring for her in her last years had been quite a burden, I think, and when she passed away there was suddenly a lightness about him, and an acceptance that there were other ways of living a life.

I'd been particularly nervous about how he might respond to the people at Tui, but he immediately fitted in. And I mean straight away. He arrived just as the lunch gong sounded, with everyone gathered in the customary circle to share thanks for the meal, walked right into the middle, and began to address everyone as if he was on a marae. He said he was looking forward to getting to know each and every one of the community, and that he was keen to contribute. I thought, 'Who is this man, and what's he done with my father?'

In the following weeks, Dad got involved in all the garden working bees, whether I was there or not. And he baked! He'd always loved baking, and had hundreds of recipes memorised – he once told me that he had 200 recipes for muffins alone. We found some old-fashioned heavy-duty baking trays in a Tākaka second-hand store, and every day he made muffins and took them around people's cottages and caravans, inviting himself in for cups of tea. He did it all using honey and wholemeal flour – foreign substances for him – modifying his recipes by feel to come up with the perfect alternative lifestylers' muffin. Next came layered sponge cakes, tarts and other treats. Soon all the kids wanted to get involved. Dad would prep the kitchen, and when they got back from school they'd have a massive bake-up. He was like the Pied Piper.

Maybe I shouldn't have been surprised. Back in Waimauku, Dad had formed a friendship with a group of Hare Krishnas after they arrived at the farm looking for a regular supply of milk. They invited him to their feasts, and they would leave treats at the milking shed when they came to fill their bottles.

While Dad was in the Bay, I thought I'd take him to see a couple of tramping huts, figuring it might give him a better sense of what made me tick. At the very least, we'd enjoy a walk together. We started with Brown Hut, 500 metres in from the Heaphy Track trailhead near the Aorere River. We arrived to find a team of possum hunters waiting for the fire to die down before heading out to check their traps. One of them told us to help ourselves to billy tea and biscuits, which blew Dad away. We sat there while it pissed down outside, eating gingernuts by the fire, Dad wearing a happy grin.

A week later we walked from the end of Cobb Dam Road for a night at Trilobite Hut. It's a very basic 12-bunk hut with a concrete floor and rumpty old mattresses, but, a bit like me, Dad was fascinated by any form of basic shelter, and he enjoyed this hut. Even better, that afternoon it started to snow, which was a whole new experience for my North Aucklander father. I have a photo of him outside the hut in a snow flurry, looking completely delighted, telling me that the snow wasn't nearly as cold as he'd expected. In the end, these simple pleasures were all it took to connect with Dad. I thought, 'Why didn't I know this earlier? Why did it take us so long?'

He left Golden Bay with a new appreciation of the choices I'd made, particularly my decision to settle at Tui. Whenever he called me afterwards, he'd engage in long, in-depth talks with whomever picked up the communal phone. Shortly before he died, I arranged a second visit, including a helicopter trip to one of my favourite backcountry huts in the Kahurangi and a flight to Karamea. Unfortunately he didn't get to do it, but it had given him a lot of excitement all the same. When I met his RSA mates at the funeral, they told me he'd been hugely looking forward to it.

*

Going home for the funeral was a strange mix of the familiar and the new. His body lay in state at the farmhouse for a few days before the event, and a lot of people came to see him. Earlier, I mentioned the bus disaster in 1963. Well, the children of those people who lost their lives were now the marae elders, and they came to pay their respects. It was only later, while I was going through Dad's affairs, that I discovered how heavily involved he and another Pākehā neighbour had been in encouraging those then young people to keep the marae going after the bus crash. There were a number of letters of thanks and appreciation.

Dad had several dogs, and they were all with him when he died. But there was one he was especially close to that was very upset. It was constantly scratching at the door, wanting to come into the house. We thought, 'Fine, let's see what it does', and let it in. It ran straight to his casket, stood up with its paws against the wood, looked down – and started wagging its tail off. After that, it was fine.

The day of Dad's burial forked into two distinctly different events – Māori and Pākehā. One of the elders who had been close to Dad felt strongly that he needed to call him onto the Reweti marae. Very quickly it was arranged, and on the morning of the service we Kilgours were warmly welcomed onto the forecourt by a rousing karanga, followed by waiata and speeches. We mingled with people we hadn't seen for ages, including some of my old primary school friends.

After the marae but before the official service at Henderson, we took Dad's casket in his van on a winding procession through the backroads of North Auckland to all of his favourite places, starting with the kauri forest. At Muriwai Beach, we scooped handfuls of black mineral sand into the casket. By the time we got to the funeral home, it was covered in sand, kauri and karaka leaves, as well as a couple of muddy pawprints. That service proved to be a far more buttoned-up experience, and there was a definite sense of being another number in a scheduled day of tearful farewells. My brothers and I comforted each other that at least we'd already given the old man a damn good send-off at the marae.

*

Dad's funeral was, in an odd way, life-affirming. But after returning to Tui, I slipped almost inexorably into a depression. It was awful, but at least I was now somewhat better equipped to cope than during my first brush with the black dog.

That had happened soon after I joined the air force, when an early romance ended badly. Naturally, I decided to go tramping alone for a couple of weeks. I quickly realised that being by yourself in the mountains wasn't any kind of escape.

It had all hit home in a valley called the Tūtaekurī, which appropriately enough translates as 'dog shit'. This was a time before the route was marked, and I was struggling to find my way out. It was raining incessantly, and everything I owned was sodden. When I reached the top of a cliff, I remember thinking, 'Well, why the hell not?', and threw myself at the void, only to get caught up in a branch. That brought me to my senses. I managed to clamber out, and kept struggling upwards. Finally, I came onto open tops, into bright sunshine. Looking around, I thought I had an idea of where I was. When I checked the map, sure enough I was looking down on the Hope River. So, I'd climbed out of the dogshit and ... well, you get the point. I had to laugh. But it was true, I did start to feel more hopeful.

There are a couple of things I learned from that experience and others since. Firstly, if I'm seriously depressed, I know the bush is no cure. You carry your baggage in with you, and the time you spend alone with your thoughts tends to backfire. Against that, if I'm suffering something milder, then nature is a surefire tonic for me. There's always something in the bush or the hills that brings me to an appreciative stop, whether that's an icy-clear mountain stream or a fantail flitting around my head. Once on a traverse in Fiordland, I stopped in the bush just as rain set in and buzzing around me was a random bumblebee. It's amazing how such a seemingly inconsequential event can lift your spirits.

There's a centre here in Golden Bay called Te Whare Mahana where young adults with emotional and mental health problems commit to various programmes. A friend and I used to take some of them tramping. It was wonderful to see the impression that walking in the bush and the mountains made on these young people who were otherwise so disconnected from nature. I was in Tākaka a while ago when a guy came up to me on the street. He said he'd been on one of our trips years earlier, and that it had changed his life. Obviously, it's not like that for everyone, but it shows what being in the outdoors can do for people.

I'm convinced that the mere action of walking at pace helps, too. When you're tramping you're breathing deeply, and all your senses are heightened. I like to brush through the ferns and feel them against me. Visually, everything is super-defined. Light sparkles through the bush. Sounds and smells are sharp and clear.

I know a guy who co-owns a little homebuilt airplane, and every so often he flies down to South Westland to catch up with his mates at the mouth of the Paringa River, about 20 kilometres down a valley from the highway. On his last trip I tagged along for the plane ride. We parked on a farm airstrip beside the river, and his friends arrived on a jet boat and took him away. When they left, I threw on my pack and walked up the valley for five days.

The first day was full of aches. I thought, 'What the hell has happened to me?' That night I had the best sleep, and when I woke up the pain had gone and I was feeling on top of the world. I was in a hut on the bush edge looking up past beautiful beech forest to a range of high mountains caked in snow. I came alive again.

Rewind to 1996, and in those months immediately following Dad's funeral I was in a bad way. I stopped going to communal lunches and working bees, and generally withdrew into myself. People could see what was happening and were gently caring and watchful; they supported me to go deeper into what was troubling me. That was a first for me, and I felt encouraged to finally get some professional help.

I went to see Dr Tim Ewer, a GP in Māpua said to be experienced in dealing with depression and chronic fatigue. At that time, the medical profession didn't recognise chronic fatigue, and wasn't much better on depression. Tim was a conventional doctor, but he was also open to alternative approaches, and realised these were very real problems. I saw him a few times, and found that a lot of his advice was common sense. For instance, he prescribed a day of bird-watching at the beach for me. Somehow I'd lost that ability to slow down and tune in to my surroundings; I needed a reminder and it started to work, to bring me back on track.

Cold Stream Hut, Lake Sumner Forest Park.

Chapter 18

My partner, Janet Huddleston, is originally from Nashville, Tennessee, and our first meeting had something of the country ballad about it. I was finishing up one of my favourite tramping trips through the wilderness between Kahurangi Point and the Heaphy, a real slog through rugged country to an old Ministry of Works hut at Mackay Downs. For the last half day, I was walking the Heaphy Track itself, looking for a spot where I'd camped a few times where there's an old track workers' campsite from the 1970s, a flat area with a little stream a couple of hundred metres off the trail. (There are four or five of these hidden little spots on the Heaphy; I prefer them to using the pre-booked sites because they allow for more spontaneous enjoyment of the wilderness.) It was in an area where kākā like to break branches and drop them on the track, so when I heard crashing up ahead naturally I thought, 'Ah, kākā!' Instead of parrots, however, I found a DOC hut warden kicking sticks off the track. My future partner. There is a rock cairn that marks the spot where we met, just above Aorere Shelter.

Janet told me that she'd just moved up from Fiordland and was about to start a job on the Abel Tasman at Whariwharangi Hut. She asked if I knew anyone who had a place at Wainui where she could leave her vehicle. Well, of course, I lived at Wainui, and said she could leave it at my place. The rest is history.

As our relationship blossomed, we began to talk about living together. It was clear that communal living wasn't Janet's scene. She's decisive and independent, likes making her own calls and getting on with it. Witness how she ended up in this country 30 years ago. She was on an around-the-world trip when she arrived in New Zealand. At Aoraki/ Mt Cook, she got involved in building an alpine hut (Beetham Hut, since destroyed by an avalanche), met some nice people and decided she could live here. She told herself she was going to travel the world and come back to live in New Zealand one day. She carried on her travels, and later met a Kiwi guy in Kenya, whom she married and moved with to Aotearoa. The relationship didn't last, but she put down roots.

When I thought about it, I realised that Tui was no longer a great fit for me, either. In truth I'd started to quietly drift, becoming increasingly more reclusive in my caravan up the hill. (In fact I was so out on a limb, it took the Jehovah's Witnesses eight years to find me. When they did finally pay me a visit, four JWs staggering up the rise on a hot summer afternoon, I was standing by my caravan with a spade in one hand, a dead possum in the other, wearing a hat, sandals and nothing else. They've been trying to forgive me ever since!)

Eventually, I left Tui and moved into Janet's place at nearby Rangihaeata, where we've been ever since. It's on a ridge near the coast, off the road between Tākaka and Collingwood. Part of our land is at the headwaters of the Onahau Estuary, and it tends to be underwater at spring tide. It's a wonderful habitat for fern birds, and I've established a predator-trapping programme to help them thrive.

It's a wonderful habitat for me, too. I can look one way and see the mountains, and sniff the air in the other direction and smell the sea. What a combination! We're five minutes from the water at high tide, and that's a huge attraction. I can walk up the coast and next thing I'm into the bush. We're also not far from the Tākaka aerodome, so I can happily hear small aircraft coming and going all day.

Golden Bay is a two-tribes sort of place, with a pretty obvious contrast between the farming community and alternative lifestylers, although that was perhaps starker a few decades ago.

In local woman Robby Robilliard's book about trying to farm in the Bay in the 1950s and '60s, she talks about how she felt when the first hippies and lifestylers started moving into the Bay. She had a very different attitude from some of her peers: 'Oh this is so exciting; these creative, intelligent, wonderful people are bringing new life to our community!' But a lot of others from that National-voting, conservative farming clique were far more suspicious. In the early days of the Tui Community there was a bit of ostracising by people who really didn't know us. In those situations I favoured the direct approach: invite them round for lunch.

I've always thought that a community that has every aspect of humanity in it is a balanced one. If that means there are things that challenge us, what's wrong with that? But Golden Bay is changing. Land prices are climbing, and that can change the nature of a place. The people who feel drawn here can't afford it, and the ones who can afford to buy houses only use them for two weeks of the year. Even so, there's still quite a cross-section and for the most part we muddle along together okay. You get a natural disaster or a bad fire, and people quickly forget their superficial differences. The classic case is a big whale rescue on Farewell Spit. A local joke starts with two whales swimming off the coast of Golden Bay. One says, 'I can sense a bit of discord in the community.' The other replies, 'Me, too. Let's strand immediately!' People pull together.

I've been in the Bay more than three decades now. I tell people that must mean I'm close to becoming a local, and somebody always responds, 'Not so fast, Paul.' But what makes a local, anyway? Some people move here and immediately they're part of the volunteer fire brigade and signed up for Search and Rescue and doing Meals on Wheels. That would qualify you, surely?

Forks Hut, Windon Burn, Southland.

Chapter 19

One of the passions Janet and I found we shared was for Antarctica. As a kid I was fascinated by Scott and Shackleton. These days we download everything you can possibly want to know about a place before we even get near the airport, but they were genuine explorers heading into the unknown. I loved those stories and I used to wonder how I could possibly get down to The Ice – hence that Erebus flight I nearly took.

Janet didn't wonder, she went. As of last count, she's worked 11 seasons in Antarctica, mostly at US bases. She worked a season at Palmer Station on the Antarctic Peninsula, nine seasons at McMurdo and one season at Patriot Hills. She was a cleaner, waste technician, radio operator, forklift operator, worked in a carpentry shop, in supply and at a remote field camp in charge of adventure tourists. She once stayed two weeks at the South Pole, helping with resupply.

In 2005, she helped me get a job at McMurdo for the four-month summer season. It was with a Kiwi supply company that had been contracted by the Americans. The firm employed five staff from New Zealand every year, and I got the job of dealing with parts to service the LC-130 ski-planes the Yanks use. As resupply officer, every time a part became unserviceable it was my job to get it off The Ice and source a replacement.

I flew there on an American C-17. As an aviation nut, that feels pretty lucky, to be able to say I've flown in a C-17. On the way down we had a briefing from a guy with a died-in-the-wool Southern drawl. It included information about what we were supposed to do if we had to land in the sea. He said, 'As far as I'm concerned, you gotta be a goddamned idiot if you step out of this plane in the Antarctic sea!'

I worked on what they called the 'second day shift', which meant that sometimes I got to drive a 4WD out to Williams Field airfield on the McMurdo Ice Shelf. That was special. You were miles from anywhere, in the shadow of the volcano. Mt Erebus is active and there was always a plume rising, evidence of some immense energy stirring out of sight – you felt like a living entity was watching over you. I savoured that sight, and I quickly grew to love the landscape. People who talk about Antarctica as a 'world of white' have got it wrong. It's like when you glance at a tūī bird and it appears to be almost entirely black; when you're tuned in to the Antarctic landscape, you start to see tones of blue, grey, green and other colours. The Americans operate a programme for artists to work in Antarctica. When I was there we had a father and son from Alabama, one of whom painted in oils, the other in watercolours. They both said the colour they brought the most of and used the least was white.

I found the place inspiring, and it struck me as crazy that there were people at McMurdo who did their entire months-long stints without once stepping outside the base. They were totally disconnected from their surroundings, living in an artificial bubble. Whenever I got an opportunity and the weather allowed, I'd be out of that place, wandering far and wide. I'd walk over the sea ice to Scott Base, or go via Observation Hill, the one with the nine-foot wooden cross at the top in memorial to Scott's party. Before breakfast or after dinner, I'd take a walk up there. The Americans had a bunch of rules about that; we were instructed to keep to the track, up and down. Happily, I had scored a New Zealand coat – the Americans have red coats, the Kiwis have blue – and I'd throw that on before I set out. I'd get adventurous and find new ways down the other side to Scott Base.

The longest walk Janet and I did together was the five-hour Castle Rock Loop. Every hour or so we'd come across little fibreglass dome-shaped survival structures with heavily insulated walls, somewhere to shelter if the wind came up. Another time we got a lift out on a supply parts vehicle to Williams Field with the idea of walking back to base. When we got out there it was getting warm, so I stuffed my down jacket, insulated trousers and multiple layers of polyprops into my pack and started hiking in a pair of shorts and a sunhat. For the first half-hour it stayed hot and windless – the marker flags that line all the roads in Antarctica were hanging limp. It didn't last. When I looked ahead, I saw some distant flags were being blown near horizontal – a very big wind was heading our way. Luckily, there was a broken-down vehicle on the side of the road. We clambered in just as the wind hit, and put on every piece of gear we could muster. I'm not sure how we would have managed that in the blizzard, but it wouldn't have been pleasant.

The only aspect of Antartica that I struggled with was having 24 hours of light. Never seeing the sun set or rise was just strange. We had blackout windows in our bedrooms to create a sense of night, but you do start to suffer from sensory deprivation down there – and, man, did I miss the green of the Kahurangi bush.

Living on an American base I could have experienced a kind of cultural deprivation, too, so I spent a lot of my downtime at Scott Base. At the entrance was a sign saying 'Kia Ora, Welcome!' That felt good. Physically, Scott Base was a lot more inviting, too. McMurdo was described to me as looking like a run-down mining town, which was about right. It had a number of bars you could socialise in but they had no windows, whereas from the Scott Base lounge you looked out to a vista of land ice meeting sea ice. I'd sit there and plug into Radio NZ, read the *Listener* or an old copy of the *Press*. I wrote a lot of letters, too, which were sent out into the world with a Ross Dependency postage stamp.

McMurdo's saving grace was its terrific recycling centre – they called it Skua Central, after the bird – which was stacked with bins of unwanted clothing. Janet and I knew quite a few families in Golden Bay who were just scraping by, and we sent boxes of stuff to our friends back there. I also retrieved a neoprene balaclava for myself to wear when I was jogging.

*

As a veteran hut-bagger, I was eager to visit Antarctica's historic explorer bases. Unfortunately, I got bumped from a group trip to Shackleton's expedition HQ at Cape Royds, but I was able to check out Discovery Hut at Hut Point, just a few hundred metres from McMurdo. Built in 1902 during Scott's first expedition to Antarctica, it's a smaller and less successful shelter than the hut built at Cape Evans on the later *Terra Nova* Expedition, the one that's generally known as 'Scott's Hut'. It was difficult to heat and the *Discovery* party ended up sleeping on the ship and using the hut for storage and drying and repairing gear. Even so, it came in handy as a staging post for three subsequent expeditions, including Shackleton's.

The hut was square and had a pyramidal timber roof – you don't need roofing iron in a place with no rain. Compared with one of our backcountry huts, the roof wasn't as steep but it was much larger and overhung an Aussie-style open verandah. Despite its supposed faults, from the outside the hut seemed soundly constructed and had withstood the test of time pretty well, all those years of blizzards and the weight of snow.

It was dark inside, but my eyes soon adjusted. Everything seemed to be stained with what I guess was smoke from the seal oil lamps and stove. It caked the walls and caught in the nose. Odours don't die in Antarctica, so I was literally smelling history. From a tiny room where they stored hay for the ponies, I caught a whiff of feed and leather harness gear.

The hut felt dry and well preserved. You touched weather-beaten pieces of timber that had seen decades of windblast and snow and they were still beautiful. On some hooks hung heavy woollen tweed clothing; tin food containers were neatly stacked against walls, the labels still visible, along with original skis and snowshoes.

It was just me and a woman from the Antarctic Heritage Trust visiting, and with no distractions I could let my mind roam. I thought about the remoteness they experienced. When the hut was constructed there were so many unknowns. What were they prepared for? What did they not realise before leaving home? Did they know for sure they'd be able to feed their dogs? A friend in Twizel who's worked with dogs in Antarctica since the 1960s told me that to feed his team of 12 dogs over one year they had to kill 200 seals.

*

I left Antarctica after four months. It had been a terrific adventure, but I had some mixed feelings about what we were doing down there, and the scale of our intervention on The Ice. A third of the population down there are scientists, and everyone else seems to be there to look after them. I had to wonder, what's that science achieving to justify our presence? Are we overdoing things? Antarctica is our last chance to keep an environment relatively pristine; it would be very easy to stuff it up.

When I exited the plane at Christchurch Airport it was dark night and hosing down, two phenomena that I hadn't experienced for four months. I stood on the tarmac in the rain for a long time taking it in, savouring the scent of wet earth.

Me (left) at age eight, with my brother Barry, Waimauku, 1959. About to head off to school. 'Let's get on with it!' The photo was taken by my father, Bob Kilgour.

These photos were taken while I was in the Air Force, in 1971 (left) and 1972 (right). It felt very foreign to me to be wearing longs, let alone a uniform!

This was my great-grandmother's bach in Waimauku – her full-time dwelling in the 1950s and 1960s. This is what got me fascinated in huts. You didn't need much: one room at the front, a kitchen at the back, a long drop in the bush, and a hand basin on the side of the bach for any washing. These photos were taken in 2002.

Baches by the Onahau River, near my home in Golden Bay, typical of the baches that featured in my younger days exploring. They are now what you might call an 'endangered species'.

My first overnight tramp, with Steve Harre (left), at White River in the Waimakariri Valley, Arthur's Pass National Park, 1972. I wouldn't have quite been 21. I'd been reading about tramping for a long while, but to actually do it for the first time – absolutely fantastic! With the first few crunches on the track, I thought, 'This is what I am going to do for the rest of my life.' When you live north of Auckland, you don't have mountains handy, so this was a transformative experience. The hut, unfortunately, is long gone. Although any removed hut is unfortunate in my mind! Everything is an asset.

Where we really 'ground our teeth'. Top Wairoa Hut, Richmond Ranges, September 1974.

On a working bee for the New Zealand Forest Service, Lower Goulter Hut, Mt Richmond Forest Park, 1974. That's me crouching down on the ground, without my shirt. Richmond Range is where I started taking tramping a lot more seriously.

Me inside the Marlborough Tramping Club hut beside Gosling Stream, beneath the Bounds Range, Waihopai Valley, 1978.

LEAVING HUT
ASE ENSURE

Urquharts Hut, Wilberforce River valley, 1976. Our Marlborough group tramping trip had been caught in a blizzard, and it was so cold that one of the party got hypothermia. This hut was certainly a welcome sight in a storm, even though it had a gravel floor!

Tasman Saddle Hut, January 1977. The Tasman Glacier is to the right, and just peeking out in the background is Mt Cook. This was taken just before my biggest climb, Mt Elie de Beaumont, at 3109 metres tall.

Slaty Creek Hut, Westland, 1977.

Turkeys Nest Bivvy, at the
headwaters of the Wye River,
Marlborough, late 1970s.

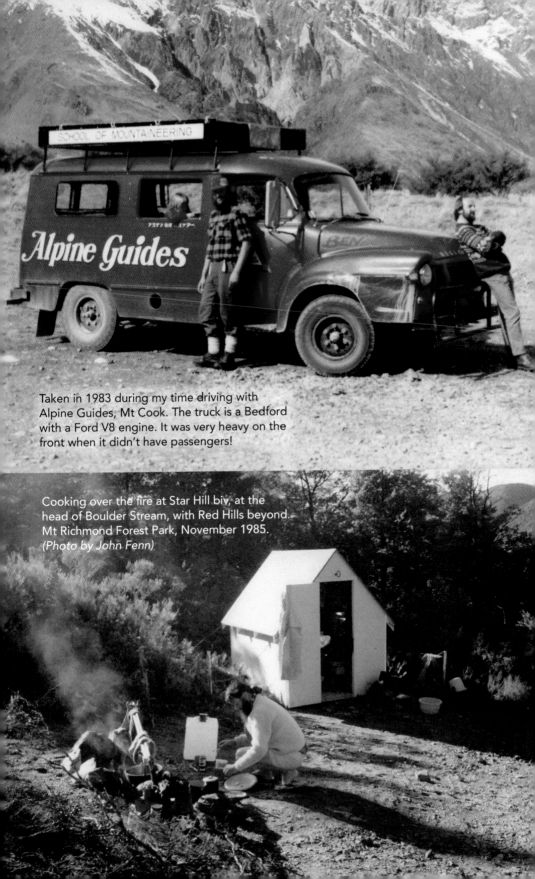

Taken in 1983 during my time driving with Alpine Guides, Mt Cook. The truck is a Bedford with a Ford V8 engine. It was very heavy on the front when it didn't have passengers!

Cooking over the fire at Star Hill biv, at the head of Boulder Stream, with Red Hills beyond. Mt Richmond Forest Park, November 1985. *(Photo by John Fenn)*

Gosling Hut, July 1990. After that trip, I decided gum boots weren't a great option for walking upriver! Even though they're easy to empty if water gets in.
(Photo by Sue Shotton)

Me with DOC ranger (and my future partner!) Janet Huddleston, at the mouth of the Heaphy River, January 2000.

Westies Hut, Prices Harbour, South Coast track, March 1999. I stayed here on the third night of my big walk home – my journey on foot from Puysegur Point at the bottom of the South Island, to Golden Bay at the top of the South Island.

Jacks Hut, Arthur's Pass, 2005. It's more of a bach, technically! Those were the days you could just go and build a bach for a peppercorn lease. The angled walls are to keep the snow away from the side of the building.

Scott Base, in the summer of 2005/2006. I lived and worked four kilometres away at the US Antarctic research station, McMurdo Station. During the four months I lived there, I'd visit Scott Base regularly.

On Hardy Ridge, off the Haupiri Range, Kahurangi National Park, October 2008. *(Photo by Clair Fones)*

North West Bay Hut, Campbell Island, January 2011. It's so far south that the alpine shrubs start just above sea level. *(Photo by Janet Huddleston)*

Castaway depot Stella Hut, down in the Screaming Sixties on Enderby Island, off Auckland Island, January 2011. These huts were originally constructed for shipwrecked sailors. The depots had basic dry food, muskets, tobacco and pipes, so marooned sailors could 'survive' while they waited to be rescued.

Kime Hut, Tararua Forest Park, September 2011. Some people call it 'the Ice Box' … it was very cold inside! But at least it was shelter from a storm. The marker poles are there to guide people to the hut in inclement weather. It can close in quickly in the Tararuas – I can understand why so many people get lost there.

On the slopes of Mt Gibbs, at the head of Cobb Valley, September 2008. (Photo by Gaylene Wilkinson)

Round Hill Hut, Kairuru Farm, Takaka Hill, December 2013.

On Needles Eye saddle, looking down into the north branch of the Anatoki River, November 2020. *(Photo by Clair Fones)*

Antarctica.

Chapter 20

Antarctica must have given me a taste for hostile southern climes – a few years later, Janet and I signed up for a trip to the Subantarctic Islands to celebrate my sixtieth year.

We travelled down as part of a Heritage Expeditions voyage. Initially, we'd considered going with DOC to do some voluntary work on the islands, but the department had introduced a 'contribution'. It was $6000 – to do some weeding! I thought our chance was gone, but then I saw an ad in *New Zealand Geographic* offering a trip at just over half the price and with three places left. So without much notice, we departed Bluff on the Russian-crewed *Spirit of Enderby* for nine days.

I'd worried about a rough boat trip down, but I needn't have. According to one of the guides on board, a guy who'd done a lot of work on the Subantarctic Islands in the 1960s and '70s, we struck the calmest conditions since 1959. There were dolphins riding our bow wave, we had barbecues on the deck and I was walking around barefoot. When we got to the islands I realised just how spoiled we were. Some of the harbour entrances that were supposed to be too dangerous for boats to enter in a big blow were a fair bit wider than Tory Channel. You could only imagine such rough conditions and shiver.

The ship had a brilliant atmosphere. Whenever we went up to the bridge the Russian captain would enthusiastically show us exactly where we were on his chart – even if it was the middle of the ocean. Those of us who were interested were also invited to see the engine room. We went down a ladder to find an immaculate scene, not a drop of oil to be seen, every moving part colour-coded. Beaming behind a glass screen in a little air-conditioned cabin was a very proud Russian engineer.

We were admiring all this neatness when I spotted something in a corner behind some wire netting. And there it was: a messy shed, with a working bench strewn with nuts and bolts and random nails, loose jars of washers, scattered tools. The engineer didn't speak much English, but when he saw me looking he came over: 'You like? You like?' I sure did. At the heart of this highly organised, beautifully run ship was a quintessential bloke's shed.

At Snares Island, we Zodiac-cruised the inlets, hearing the noisy bray of endemic Snares crested penguins lining the shore. From there, we sailed for 30 hours through rough seas to Campbell Island, where we woke to a view of near-vertical cliffs, the air full of soaring albatrosses. At the other end of the island we entered a natural harbour – apparently it was one of very few times the captain had found it calm enough to get the boat in there, so we felt very lucky.

There was a small medical drama soon after we arrived. A DOC scientist from the nearby base had been bitten by a sea lion and was rushed out to see the ship's doctor. This guy had been studying sea lions for more than 20 years, I believe, and this was the first time that he'd been bitten. On the Subantarctic Islands, the sea lions often sleep hidden from sight among thick vegetation, and he'd stepped on one while walking through some long tussock grass. It was a timely warning for us about the risks of walking around the island.

The islands were magnificently forbidding when viewed from the sea. But once ashore, we began to appreciate some of the subtle peculiarities of the subantartic environment. The megaherbs, for instance, are like perennials on steroids, with long strap-like leaves and prodigious flowers, and they were in full bloom. On Campbell, we walked among fields of vivid yellow Ross lilies and pink Campbell Island carrots. Auckland Island, meanwhile, was ringed by flowering rātā from sea level all the way to the alpine environment – which was only about 20 metres! (That close proximity was fascinating, and like nothing I'd experienced.)

We did an eight-hour hike on Campbell and a six-hour walk on Enderby, in the Auckland Islands, and it wasn't nearly enough. The wildlife was incredible. We saw 14 different types of albatross, watched them land with a thump and fold in their wings like origami. We saw birdlife unknown on mainland New Zealand – the Auckland Island snipe, for example, which is about the size of a thrush with a long beak, and the Campbell Island teal. Birds that are rare on mainland New Zealand were sitting around in numbers, while familiar species had subtly different colouring.

We saw sea lions, too, of course, but also elephant seals and even a leopard seal. You'd look along a stony beach and see what looked to be a large grey rock – no, it's a very still elephant seal! We realised they were aware of us long before we were aware of them. In one place we were walking through head-high hebes when suddenly there was a baby sea lion looking up at us. It was very cute, but we knew that its mother must be nearby, even possibly watching us, so we quickly backtracked. There was also, sadly, evidence of doomed early efforts to farm the islands – wild rabbits, pigs, the usual legacy of thoughtless human habitation. That will take a while yet to undo.

The historic huts were easier to enjoy – at least for me. On Campbell Island, I bagged my southernmost huts – Tucker Cove and Northwest Bay. The latter was a five-hour slog through rugged country and along clifftops to the western side of the island, and was still being used by scientists studying subantarctic birdlife – it was nicknamed the Penguin Café. At Auckland Island's Ranui Cove, we visited the relics of a base that had been established in the Second World War for coast-watchers, people who were sent down there to watch for enemy ships. Poor buggers. Imagine being posted to the Subantartic Islands *just in case*. You had a hunting rifle to defend yourself or a cave to hide in if you ever actually saw an invader.

The coast-watchers had it cushy, though, compared with the shipwrecked, of which there were potentially hundreds – between 1860 and the early 1900s boats were crashing into these remote and tiny islands at the rate of one shipwreck every five years. It must have been sheer hell to be a castaway at this latitude, blasted by blizzards and snow, waiting for a ship to appear. On the trip down I read an account of two groups that survived for a year before being rescued, each unaware that there was a second bunch clinging to life on the other side of the island.

At some point in the 1870s, someone had the bright idea of building a series of 'castaway depots' at likely spots around the islands. These were little A-framed weatherboard shelters for storing caches of survival provisions, including food, matches, tobacco and pipes, muskets and ammunition. Everything was packed into animal-proof drums, and the doors were set low and tight as a further deterrent to pilfering sea lions. On Enderby Island we followed a series of historic fingerposts to Stella Hut (1880), one of the earliest and most complete of the depots.

Humans weren't the only castaways: on the Campbell Island coastline we saw what must be the world's loneliest conifer tree. It had been planted to have something to decorate at Christmas, but in the acidic soils had never grown beyond head height. For me that summed up what Subantartic Island life must have been like.

Antarctica.

Chapter 21

In 2008, I took on a two-week voluntary conservation job at Coal Island/Te Puka-Hereka, off Puysegur Point at the southern head of Preservation Inlet. This is Fiordland's southernmost fiord, where the only access is by sea, air or on foot, and you really do feel out on a limb.

I'd been invited by the South West New Zealand Endangered Species Charitable Trust, which was established in the early 2000s to create a wildlife sanctuary on Coal Island. My job was to check on the hundreds of traps on the island, as well as another line of traps running down Preservation Inlet to Puysegur Point. At night, we stayed at Kisbee Lodge on the mainland. It was built to be an exclusive tourist lodge, but became a bit of a white elephant and is now a flash hunting lodge and base camp for the Trust.

The landscape and weather in that part of New Zealand is formidable, and the human history is equally raw: impenetrable bush, endless rain, multiple shipwrecks. But to my surprise I found Preservation Inlet was beautiful. The lodge caretaker loaned me a little runabout boat and in my downtime I explored the bays. I recall idyllic sandy beaches bookended by rugged headlands, with hills that rose almost vertically.

*

I'd decided before leaving home that when I'd finished the two weeks, I was going to walk back from Puysegur Point to Golden Bay, which is close to the length of the South Island. 'Paul's Big Walk Home', as someone labelled it early on, was to be an 800-kilometre odyssey as the crow flies, but much further than that on foot, through every kind of weather and terrain the South Island had to offer. It was the big one, potentially a 100-day tramp, although I'd made a decision early on that I wasn't going to set myself an ETA, but concentrate on enjoying the process and the moment.

Why do it? To quote Mallory on Everest, 'because it's there'. This was public land – *our* land. And there were so many parts of it that I'd flown over and just itched to explore. I wanted to get down there in the flax and the tussock of unknown country, to see it up close with a pack on my back.

In fact, I'd pitched the idea to my air-force superiors as far back as the 1970s. I figured I would get leave without pay and go walking. Frustratingly, the guy with the final say, and who really had zero appreciation of my style of tramping, said, 'No, sorry, walking in the mountains on your own is far too dangerous', and that sank it. But I'd never let the idea go, and when I got the Trust's email inviting me down south I knew this was the moment. 'Right, no excuses, if I want to do this before I turn 60, now's my chance. I'm heading to Puysegur Point and then I'm walking home.'

My preparations had been all about two things – getting intimate local knowledge of my intended route, and trying to travel light. The first was taken care of when some Te Anau friends put me in touch with a seasoned Fiordland-based helicopter pilot, Sam Gawith, to fly me in to Preservation Inlet. We met at a Te Anau café the day before the flight, and Sam pored over my maps, pointing out potential hazards and describing the terrain. He knew all the huts, too, including one that wasn't marked on any map but which he said could be a backup option on the traverse into Lake Poteriteri. I made a mental note.

As for travelling light, food was the complicating factor – it always is on longer tramps. You scrutinise product labels to the nth degree, juggling calorific value, weight and the time it will take to cook something. You never get the balance perfectly right, but modern dehydrated tramping meals help, and rice and high-energy snack bars are always on my shopping list. On this mission, although I'd organised a series of resupply stops, I'd still potentially have to carry a month's worth of grub. Thankfully, Sam had a good idea. Pointing to Lake Poteriteri on the map, he suggested we could fly by on the way to Preservation Inlet and deposit half of my food for the first leg at the lakeside hut.

That immediately lightened my load. Apart from food, a one-man tent and sleeping bag, I packed only the absolute basics – a primus and billy, GPS, compass and locator beacon, and sufficient clothing for all conditions. Rather than lugging all the relevant maps, I packed printouts of the relevant sections. It wasn't until much later in Canterbury that I reached places that I didn't have route information for, but that was fine because I knew that country pretty well. In the end I whittled everything down to 20 kilograms. It wasn't much for such a long trip, but I'd be resupplying along the way and felt confident that I had everything I needed to handle whatever the weather gods threw at me.

When the morning of departure from Puysegur Point arrived, it was a pearler – not a breath of wind and a clear sky, apart from the ubiquitous clouds of Fiordland sandflies.

Two women from the lodge, Karen and Jan, who'd been supportive during the build-up, walked with me along the beach. They asked me, 'Well, Paul, you're about to walk all the way to Golden Bay. How does it feel?' I thought about what lay ahead, and started to get a bit overwhelmed. 'Right,' I thought, 'just focus on the next step.' I turned to them and said, 'One step at a time is really good walking.' Immediately I felt a weight lift.

I farewelled Karen and Jan at the end of the beach, but I'd only gone a hundred metres when I heard a crashing sound in the bush below me. I yelled out and a voice came back, 'Gidday, is there a track up there?' So much for solitude in the wilderness!

It turned out to be a party of four from Invercargill whom we'd watched come ashore earlier. They were walking into the Wilson Mine with a very outdated map, so they tramped with me for the next few hours and we shared some lunch. At the mine, we said goodbye and I headed downriver. A John Muir line came to mind: 'Only by going alone in silence, without baggage, can one truly get into the heart of the wilderness.'

I stopped walking for a minute to soak it up. There's a wonderful feeling I sometimes get when I'm tramping, an endorphin rush that springs from the realisation that 'Here I am, this tiny creature, the only one for miles around, in a huge land'. It's hard to convey, but it was powerful in that moment. Right on cue, I looked up and saw a random one-inch aluminium marker nailed to a tree. I scratched 'Paul Kilgour, ex-Puysegur Point' on it and an arrow pointing to Golden Bay.

I'd chosen my route based on reading a few guides and various people's accounts of their trips, stitched together with places on my maps that looked intriguing. But I quickly realised that to do a straight-line run from A to B in that kind of country wasn't an option. The maps told me as much. When you see signs of sloping ground it tends to indicate that the bush is pretty dense, especially if it's also south-facing. Being constantly hit by strong winds encourages scrub to grow thick to strengthen itself – that's great for the bush, not so good for the tramper. Likewise, a particularly narrow river may well be too deep to cross.

When I combined all of those 'data points' with my instinct to travel through the most interesting country, it resulted in a rough initial route heading east via a series of Southland lakes, then turning north in the direction of Lake Wakatipu and beyond. I say rough because in that kind of landscape you have to leave your options open. You're always going to be diverting around unexpectedly steep areas or unpredictably deep rivers, avoiding gullies, or choosing an easier line uphill.

I learned early in my tramping days that in thicker bush if I saw a meandering creek I should follow it. It might appear to take you away from your intended course, but it's a good way to avoid having to bash through what I call the 'scratchy stuff', which is the kind of bush that just rips you. On this first day, I found the Grace Burn, the most beautiful little knee-deep stream I've ever encountered. I waded a long distance upstream, avoiding the roughest vegetation, and when I got to a tussock tongue I followed that, all the while sussing out how the land lay, how the bush covered the country, going with the flow.

After 12 hours' walking, I pitched camp that first night beside a tarn in tussocky subalpine country. I had company in the shape of a skua bird, a noisy reminder of just how far south I was. Unsurprisingly, it scavenged stuff as I established my camp, including my father's old fingerless woollen mittens – good nest material, no doubt.

Also unsurprisingly, I was soon being savaged by sandflies. I've alluded to these little buzzing bastards already, but they really were a menace in Fiordland – as I knew they would be. In fact, I'd set my pack up with all the snack food readily accessible in the front pockets specifically to minimise any chance of being a stationary target. When I had to stop for any length of time I'd throw on one of those insect screens that you wear like a hat to cover your face.

The night was dry and warm, and the pattern was repeated over the following days. Friends who'd tramped through the same country the previous year had encountered horrible weather and a series of treacherous river crossings. But luckily for me, the early going wasn't nearly as bad as I'd anticipated. At the mouth of Lake Kiwi, where my friends had struck such deep water that they had to find a whole new route, I crossed in water that was barely knee-deep. Likewise Big River, which I'd been sweating about since I left Puysegur Point, was at worst waist-deep. Exiting the river, I had paused to take a quick photo when I heard a loud splash. Looking upriver, I saw a massive stag, seven to eight points, swimming across the river. Weirdly, it only had one antler.

During the walk between Puysegur Point and Big River, I'd periodically come across bits of the old telephone line from Orepuki, West Southland. The authorities had once nailed porcelain insulators to trees, slashed off the tree tops, then run wires through – a massive undertaking when you consider the landscape. Now I was looking for the Southern Coastal Track, but I was finding it difficult to locate. I checked the map, crawled up through thick fern, stood again, and promptly tripped over a downed telephone wire. Yep, I'd found the track!

I'd taken three days to reach Big River, which was fast walking – the famous Moir's guidebook had estimated two weeks. But it wasn't a triumph of pace so much as about keeping ahead of the local predators. In that western part of

Southland during high summer it gets light at 4.30 am and dark at 10.30 pm, and I'd been walking all of the hours between to beat the sandflies, averaging perhaps 20 kilometres a day. Now I was ready for a breather.

It was close to 9 pm when I reached the Southern Coastal Track, but I pushed on for another hour and a half, determined to sleep that night at one of my favourite spots, the wonderful Westies Hut at Prices Harbour.

Cavalier Creek Hut, Mason Bay, Stewart Island.

Chapter 22

For years I resisted embracing the term 'hut bagger'. It had the whiff of competitive sport about it, and I've never been keen on competition. But in 2002, over a long winter with the fire blazing, I had begun to work through nearly 50 years' worth of logbooks, counting them up.

The immediate impetus was that someone who had written a letter to *Wilderness* magazine had become excited that they'd knocked off a 400th hut. To me, that seemed a little underwhelming – by then I'd visited 700 huts without even thinking about keeping score. I'd also become aware of a hut baggers' website where people were making ridiculous claims, bagging fishermen's huts just over the fence from the highway and bragging about it.

The other, more significant reason for my change of heart was that I'd realised that hut bagging might be pretty good motivation. What I call 'home-itis' had slowly crept up on me. Home can be an excuse not to do other things. I'd look up at the mountains and think, 'Oh, perhaps I'll prune the fruit trees today, or do some mulching.' Hut bagging became a spur to get out and explore fresh country and to really stretch my legs.

So, in the winter of 2002, I counted them up and found that in the previous 31 years, I'd bagged 620 huts. As mentioned, the tally now stands at 1208. They're not necessarily all huts I've stayed at, but I've cast my shadow on each and every one. (I have a second list of huts that I've seen from afar, perhaps from the air or from the other side of a raging river or the top of a bluff, that are all on the 'to-do' list.)

The northernmost hut bagged was in the Hunua Ranges, near Auckland. The southernmost was on Campbell Island, 663 kilometres south of Bluff. I've stayed in all sorts: historic musterers' huts; huts built by tramping and alpine clubs; early New Zealand Forest Service huts and contemporary Department of Conservation huts. They include shelters built from parts helicoptered or carried into the remotest of country by surveyors, deerstalkers and pig hunters. Most have been legal – but not all. Some have woven such a spell on me I wonder how I ever left them.

I love huts that are built from very basic, often recycled materials, and that do just the bare minimum to keep people safe and warm. I admire the resourcefulness and bloody-minded determination of their builders. Take those rough corrugated-iron huts in that nineteenth-century Chinese miners' settlement at Arrowtown. To think that people lived in those through several raw Central Otago winters!

The three most spectacularly sited huts I've stayed at were all in Aoraki/Mt Cook National Park. The Tasman Saddle Hut is arguably the best of them all, sited on a rocky buttress poking up at the head of the Tasman Glacier, surrounded by the park's highest peaks. It's astounding. It also has what might be the world's longest long drop – you almost had to weigh the paper down with a stone or a piece of ice to get it to the bottom!

My memories of the hut are dominated by a German guy I met there. Hans had arrived at Mt Cook Village with no background in mountaineering, no gear, and very little money, but a keen appetite for alpine adventure. Rather than fork out for appropriate clothing, he bought some wool, some knitting needles and a how-to book and started knitting. He arrived at the hut with cross-country skis, dressed head to foot in his own creations. It got better. The next morning he informed us that he was going to do something groundbreaking. He stripped down until he was wearing only a woolly hat, pack and ski boots, and skiied off downhill. What he'd failed to notice was the ski plane full of tourists that had landed further down the glacier. That was the last I saw of Hans. Love to know what his adventures in life have been since then.

*

Some huts in Aoraki/Mt Cook have met violent ends, blown off their foundations by a horrendous wind gust or undermined by glacial retreat. Mueller Hut, at 1800-odd metres in the Sealy Range, has been through four or five iterations. The one I stayed at in the 1970s was the third, I think. It was a basic 1950s or '60s construction, with a simple wooden frame, wooden floor and iron cladding, with a sleeping platform at one end and a cooking area at the other. The appeal of Mueller wasn't the architecture, it was the view, dominated by mighty Mt Sefton directly in front. As the day warmed, you'd hear thunderous avalanches up in its high slopes, and see great chunks of ice and snow break off and plummet into the Hooker and Mueller valleys. It was a hell of a show.

To climb up to Haast Hut (aka King Memorial Hut) at 2000 metres on the eastern flank of Aoraki/Mt Cook was a sometimes dicey proposition – as you might expect of a hut that was originally erected as a memorial to three climbers killed in the area in 1914. I visited the third iteration of the hut in the 1970s, and I remember clambering out of the collapsing lateral moraine thinking one slip and I'd be gone forever. From there we were into steep table country, a bit of snow around, and suddenly there was this little A-frame hut perched on a thin ridge not much bigger than the building itself, a rock buttress pressing at its back. There was a long-drop toilet and a weather station squeezed in alongside, both of which were later blown away. Inside, the platform bunk was just large enough to accommodate four sleepers.

It was an incredible place to be in a storm. Ice and loose snow falling from the face above would slide down the A-frame's tin sides, and in a big wind, it would creak and shake. I took some comfort from the fact that it had been there a long time – although I guess you could've said that of other Mt Cook huts lost over the years. In the end, it wasn't a big one-off storm but the steady ingress of snow and rain that finally did for Haast Hut, which was removed by DOC in 2018.

Spectacle and location are all very well, but when you boil it down a hut's number-one purpose is to provide shelter. I recall a hut where I hunkered down over several days of torrential rain. It barely had a door, and the water quickly found a way through cracks and fissures to flow across the rough stone floor. But my bed was high and dry and the fire was unthreatened, so I wasn't overly bothered. I had shelter from the storm.

There's a huge nostalgic buzz for me about historic backcountry huts. I always think of them as being a combination of three beautiful elements: rusty iron; weathered wood; and either stones or brick. That's the essence of a hut. By contrast, new huts often smell of building materials, paints and varnishes. I'm not a fan. Sure, I appreciate any shelter on my route, especially if there's a storm coming on. But the new DOC huts tend to lack character and charm.

Having said that, a few years ago I officially opened the then spanking-new 24-bed Perry Saddle Hut on the Heaphy Track. I wasn't supposed to be cutting the ribbon – I was attending the event as a tramping club representative. But when an unforecast snowstorm rolled in, grounding the politician who was supposed to be doing the honours, the DOC area manager asked me to step into the breach. I found a strip of red tape in my pack – I always carry tape for marking things – that fitted across the doorway, and someone produced a pair of scissors. Before I cut the thing, I gave a brief speech in which I compared the new building with the original Perry Saddle Hut, which I first visited in 1972, very soon after it was opened.

*

What are my favourite huts? That's not easy to answer. I can think of a handful that I have enjoyed immensely, but which on other occasions I couldn't wait to leave. The Kahurangi Keepers' House Hut near the lighthouse at Kahurangi Point is one of these sometime-favourites. When it's inundated by 4WDs and motorbikes and men knocking back cans of beer its charms pale and I quickly walk on.

But there are a handful of places that have never lost their appeal. The hut I've been to most is also among the most obscure. It's a historic Ministry of Works hut set among the red tussocks of Mackay Downs between the Heaphy Track and Kahurangi Point that was built in 1970 as a base for surveyors sussing out a proposed road link between Nelson and the West Coast. They only used it twice; I've visited 19 times.

What's so special about it? Well, the location for a start: Mackay Downs is incredibly difficult to get to. I had my first trip there in 1990 with a couple of friends, and it took us three attempts to get to the hut from the Heaphy Track before we finally figured out a route that didn't involve total immersion in scratchy subalpine vegetation, supplejack and swathes of cutty grass. I can do that same walk now in three hours – but only if I get the route 100 per cent right.

To get through from the coast side is even trickier. It's such complex country that you can inadvertently drop into a gully and before you know it you're totally bamboozled. The quickest I've done that route (10 hours) was walking with a group of eight others and we all had specific jobs: one person was on the map, someone else was handling compass duties, another was doing the GPS, and so on. When I've walked it solo and done all those jobs myself, my quickest time was 14 hours.

Once I camped for a night on my way to Mackay Downs and did a GPS fix. On the return leg, I stopped again and did another fix and found I was camping on exactly the same grid reference yet never recognised the spot. It's such rugged country you can be metres from where you've camped before and not recognise a thing. But that's the appeal of the hut for me – remoteness and the physical and mental challenge of reaching it.

In 2002, DOC announced it was thinking of moving the Mackay Downs hut. A bunch of us fought against the proposal. Golden Bay-based writer Gerard Hindmarsh fired off hundreds of emails to rally people to the cause, and that was followed by a well-attended meeting at St Arnaud. DOC's argument was that the hut cost the department far too much to maintain given its low usage. They said there'd been only four entries in the visitor book the previous year – and two of them were mine! I thought, 'We can play the numbers game, too.' In the next year, I encouraged, press-ganged and cajoled enough people to visit the hut that we got the number up from four to 42. At the end of the year, I highlighted the increase and said, 'Show me another hut in New Zealand that has had anything like that kind of growth!'

At the same time, I'd been pointing out the hut's historic merits, including its founding purpose as a surveyors' hut for the never-built Heaphy road and the fact that it was built of kahikatea as opposed to the usual rimu, tōtara or pine (they used kahikatea because it was lighter to carry in). As well, this six-bunk hut had never been modified – it even had its original fireplace – and apparently there was only one other six-bunker in the country that was as untouched. In the end, DOC sent in its historian to check it out, and he was overwhelmed by what he found. He wrote it up: 'huge historical significance'; 'can never be moved'; 'must be retained in original condition' – or words to that effect. We'd saved the hut.

Another Kahurangi hut that has meaning for me is at Boulder Lake, a day's walk south from the Aorere River. Again, part of the appeal of this one is its history: Boulder Lake Hut and nearby Adelaide Tarn and Lonely Lake huts were three milestones in the formation of my much-loved Golden Bay Alpine & Tramping Club. What's more, Boulder Lake Hut played a role in the creation of Kahurangi National Park, one of my favourite parts of the world.

It's a good story, that one. In 1960, a group of local botanists, farmers and trampers from Golden Bay who used to walk around in the mountains of Kahurangi decided that they needed a hut. They were told they couldn't build anything unless they were an official club, so one day at Boulder Lake they formed the Golden Bay Alpine & Tramping Club – they added the alpine bit because alpine plants were the botanists' speciality, and the name stuck. A top-dressing pilot dropped in materials and gear, and they all walked in together and built a hut.

The same people had also been campaigning for the wider area to be protected. Now that they were an official group with a hut, they sent their tidiest-looking person off to see the Minister of Lands and push the case. The Minister wanted to see the concept on paper, so they drew a line on a map from Tākaka to Karamea to Murchison to Motueka, at that moment feeling greedy to be 'grabbing' so much land. Some of those same lines now represent the borders of the Kahurangi National Park. You can feel that history when you're in there – the land surrounding you is national park because of a handful of people who made a commitment at Boulder Lake.

The original Boulder Lake Hut is still standing, although it's been superseded by a new one nearby. In this case the replacement is actually pretty lovely. It's got a terrific fire and a pair of platform bunks that sleep eight people. And it's beautifully located, right on the bush edge with a view across the lake. I love just hanging out at Boulder Lake Hut, enjoying the surroundings.

Nearby Adelaide Tarn Hut was built by the same tramping club pioneers as Boulder Lake, who created a route through to the Cobb Valley via the Dragon's Teeth. Even today when you walk from Boulder Lake to Adelaide, you can still see the homemade route markers they put up – old preserving-jar lids with thumbnail-sized reflective stickers in the middle. We call them 'Marshall markers' after Murray Marshall, who made them. It's a cute hut, as is Lonely Lake

Hut, which was built by the Forest Service in 1972 with a lot of input from the tramping club. In the last few years, a group of Golden Bay people got funding through the Backcountry Hut Trust to restore it. They put in insulation and an additional window and painted it blue and yellow. It's brilliant: you stare into the bush wondering 'Where's the toilet?', and spy a bright daffodil-yellow door.

Being so close to home, I've visited all three of those huts many times. There are other huts, however, where I may have stayed just once but I've never forgotten them. There's something about them – it just feels good to be there – or perhaps I've enjoyed something out of the ordinary, like hearing a kiwi call in the night or seeing a native falcon flying overhead or having kea visit. Other huts, you think, 'What a grotty hole; who'd want to stop here any longer than they had to?' Yet another time I'd arrive at that same hut in a downpour, grateful to have a place to shelter, and it would have a totally different feel.

There was once a hut I literally walked into in the dark. I was walking from Tākaka to Murchison through the Kahurangi park. I'd just left Fenella Hut in the Cobb Valley and had gone over the tops on my first-ever trip into the Roaring Lion River, a tributary of the Karamea. As soon as I got to the river it started hosing down. It was nearly dark, and the ground was becoming wet and swampy so I headed away from the river to find a place to camp for the night. I was poking around in the bush in the dark and suddenly I walked into something. A big sheet of vertical plastic – the wall of a hut. It was a basic structure, iron on the roof and four walls made of plastic and a piece of plywood you pulled aside as the door. But it had a fireplace, a modified 44-gallon drum. At the very moment I needed it, I walked into a hut I didn't know existed.

That was 1987. Two years ago I was dropping someone off at Nelson Hospital and bumped into a guy I know, a hunter. We started talking about some of the huts that he and other hunters had built in the Kahurangi National Park, and I learned that there are about 14 'illegal' huts out there. He started talking about one he'd built near the Roaring Lion River that the department had quickly pulled down. I realised that it was the hut I'd bumped into all those years ago. He was thrilled to know it had provided me shelter at a time I needed it.

*

If a hut is particularly remote or obscure, I'm keen to see it. There's a good example on the Grange Ridge in the Kahurangi high above Beautiful River that was built for a group monitoring endangered rock wrens. A friend involved with the monitoring programme once gave me the grid reference and challenged me to go find it. I told him, 'Actually, I walked up there two years ago.' He congratulated me, then set another challenge, giving me a grid reference for a little hut in the upper Roaring Lion that's used for kiwi watching. I said, 'Mate, I've already got my eye on that one.'

I'm a fan, too, of the hunters' huts of Stewart Island. In the days before they were built, hunters would boat or chopper in to their favourite remote spot, cut down tree saplings and construct basic shelters using sheets of plastic. And that was fine, but often they'd leave plastic and other rubbish behind. A group of Stewart Islanders thought, 'Let's build some proper huts so they don't have to bring this junk in.' There was a bit of resistance at first, but today the Rakiura Hunter Camp Trust has got 14-odd huts scattered around the remote reaches of the island. There's also a Rakiura Māori Lands Trust that has built even more.

I stayed in one of those huts while helping DOC on a coastal clean-up and I'm keen to see more. In fact, I've spoken to both trusts about doing a circuit of them, perhaps during a winter window when the hunting season's finished and I can have the island largely to myself. They're very basic six-bunkers, just a sloped roof on a rectangle, and built of plywood. They tried to keep costs down to about $30,000, and local boat and helicopter operators helped by donating their services. Sadly, as is too often the case, council regulations have made it far more expensive to build any new ones.

*

We have a habit of over-regulating the backcountry – the 'Handrails in the Mountains' scenario. Everything is going great, then someone decides we need a safety plan. Even little two-bunk huts on DOC land now require a fire safety plan, including a sign on the hut wall explaining what to do in a fire and another sign showing where the exit is. Well, I'd think it's pretty obvious, isn't it? You use the door and you get the hell out of there! When I made enquiries a few years ago, those fire plans cost $1500.

There's something lacking in the common-sense department, and it's led to the removal of far too many historic huts – in my opinion, unnecessarily. I've mentioned the first backcountry hut I bagged, the White River Hut in the Arthur's Pass area, which I visited on my first overnight tramping trip in 1972. Nearby was the Canterbury Mountaineering Club's Carrington Hut. Both have since been removed – the Carrington Hut was replaced by a massive thing, one of the country's largest DOC huts – victims of a drive to 'rationalise the hut system'.

Thank goodness for the Permolat group, which has saved more than 100 huts by undercutting the arguments for their removal. The group is named after the aluminium trail markers used back in the day by the Forest Service and it has a number of branches – there's one in Southland, another that is looking out for the huts of the Ruahine Ranges, and there's a very active one on the West Coast, along with several others. It's all voluntary, and some businesses help by donating materials, paint, food and services such as helicopter transport.

One of our tactics has been to encourage more people to visit these threatened huts so no one can say they're surplus to requirements. As well, we've started to give these shelters regular and expert TLC, so it also can't be argued that they're a drain on the public purse. I've helped with maintenance in the Hokitika conservancy at huts near the Waitaha River and off the Haupiri River, inland from Greymouth. I've also tried to do my bit in an indirect way. For instance, people involved in hut restoration often put out requests on the Permolat website for specific building materials – some tōtara or rimu tongue-and-groove flooring, say – and I've got a lot of that stuff stashed at home. In the case of Stoney Creek Hut near Queenstown, someone wanted some timber to restore the flooring around the fireplace and I was able to find the perfect pieces in my stash.

Sometimes these huts are too far gone for restoration and require a major rebuild. The complication is that DOC's position only allows for 'like to be replaced with like', but that can be worked around. For example, when a little bivvy in Arthur's Pass was falling down, someone came up with a proposal to save it. Within a week, volunteers and materials were assembled. They flew in on Friday, and by Saturday the hut was demolished except for two original foundation posts. It was then rebuilt using 'like for like' materials – all new, of course.

Pinnacle Bivvy, Hokitika area.

Chapter 23

Back to Westies Hut – so named because for eight years it was the home of Southland legend Owen West, of whom you'll hear more later. By the time I arrived at Prices Harbour on my long walk from Puysegur Point to Golden Bay it was dark, and I had to find the hut by following Westie's old handmade signs by torchlight. There was no one there, so I took the main hut, with a window looking out to the roaring sea just metres away.

I've talked about spectacularly located huts. Well, Westies is a unique entry in that category, being sited in a cavernous, multi-exit uplifted sea cave 15 metres above the high-tide mark. Westie, a former commercial fisherman, 'inherited' the original hut from a Southland crayfisherman when it was even more rudimentary, just a light aluminium frame with some canvas, plus a door that was reportedly salvaged off a wrecked fishing boat. He proceeded to give it a Southland makeover, using materials gifted by the sea, adding a stove, bench, sink, bed and other creature comforts. To seal it from draughts, he lined the walls and ceiling with wallpaper. Later, he built a new four-bunk bunkhouse alongside for passing trampers.

After Westie moved on, DOC signalled it planned to remove the abandoned hut because it didn't meet the department's onerous standards. Luckily a group of Southland outdoorspeople committed to upgrading it. The restorers temporarily removed the very much non-DOC-sanctioned wallpaper to put in fire-retardant insulation, then put the wallpaper back – thank goodness, because it makes Westies one of the cosiest huts you'll ever visit.

Next morning, I was fossicking on the beach when a fishing boat motored in close. A voice called out, 'Are you Paul Kilgour?' 'Yep!' 'You all good?' 'I'm fine.' 'Okay, great. Meri said to keep an eye out for you.' Meri Leask, the so-called 'Voice of Bluff', is a volunteer marine radio operator. From her home overlooking Bluff Harbour she keeps tabs on commercial and recreational fishing boats in Southland waters – she's been doing it for decades, answering distress calls and keeping people safe. Before I set out on my big walk home, I'd called her to let her know what I was planning and my route. She said, 'Oh good to know; you're now on the list to mention to anybody in the area.'

Later, there were occasions when a helicopter would fly close overhead and the pilot would give me a quizzical thumbs up. That was Meri's work again. I found it reassuring to know that locals were aware of me and, without intruding on my experience of the wilderness, were keeping an eye out for me.

As an aside, whenever I set out on a big walk I relay my intentions to someone – my 'safety person' – and set a date for when they should start thinking about raising the alarm. These are people who know the lay of the land and who aren't inclined to panic. That's a big rule of mine: never pass on your walking intentions to people who have a tendency to freak out.

While packing to leave Prices Harbour, I contemplated my options for the day ahead. On a previous tramp, Westie had told me about a coastal shortcut he used from his camp to the Waitutu River. On that occasion I gave it a crack, and it had turned out to be very tricky going. There'd been a few bluffs to climb, and at one point I had to crawl through a coastal cave that was slippery with kelp, keeping an eye out for seals. This time, I decided to play it safe and stick to the overgrown Southern Coastal Track.

I reached the mouth of the Waitutu River late in the morning, and paused before heading inland. This would be my last sighting of the sea until I reached Golden Bay many weeks hence. I decided to mark the moment with a quick plunge into the brisk Southland waters.

Working my way upriver, I was forced by rough weather to take a rest day at Slaughterburn Hut. This was the 'mystery hut' that Sam Gawith had shown me on my map back in Te Anau. (Years after my visit, I heard the hut was undermined by the Slaughterburn River, and condemned. DOC has now built a replacement a little further up the valley. I'll have to bag that one, too.) There were four people there who had walked in from the Waitutu Hut using a track that I'd never heard of. They'd taken four hours, I'd taken eight. Well, I had to take my hat off to them, they knew their backcountry. One of the guys showed me a quick route through to Lake Poteriteri that included three swing bridges that weren't even marked on the map.

A day later, I'd worked my way upriver to Lake Poteriteri and found the hut where I'd stashed food on the chopper flight to Preservation Inlet. Poteriteri is a stunner, so when the next morning dawned still and warm I decided to take a rest day and explore. I headed up the side of the lake, wading through chest-deep water around a couple of bluffs then drying out on a sandy beach. As far as I could tell, I had the entire lake to myself.

I love rest days. They're a chance to have a good wash and to clean and repair my gear. If it's an enforced stop to take shelter from a storm, I'll hunker down by the fire and write up my notebooks. If the weather's good, I'll sometimes take a side trip for a few hours to check out new country, but generally it's all about recharging my batteries. I'll get up when I feel like it, eat when I need to, and go with the flow. I always write the same thing in the hut book: 'How good it is to do nothing all day long, and then, having done so, to relax. PS: today was a rest day!'

There was sad coda to that day at Poteriteri, however. As I read through the hut book, I found references to a 1999 helicopter crash that had claimed the life of a pilot I knew, Trevor Green, and four passengers. I'd met Trevor when I was doing a beach clean-up on Stewart Island; he flew us from Ruggedy Beach to Colic Bay. Days later, I was cooking dinner at a hut near Big River when Trevor arrived with a party of hunters. I remember he cracked a joke about me popping up everywhere, then asked after a couple of Canadian trampers he'd dropped in a day earlier – he wanted to know that they were safe, which impressed me.

At the time of the crash, Trevor had just flown in half of a tight-knit group of friends to Poteriteri for a hunting trip. He was bringing in the second lot when there was a 'sudden loss of control' – speculation was that he'd possibly had a heart attack – and the chopper hit trees in the Alton Valley. The first group endured an awful night at the hut wondering what had happened, before getting the news. In the hut book, they'd written heartfelt tributes to their dead mates.

From Poteriteri, the plan was to tramp north-east to Teal Bay, at the bottom of neighbouring Lake Hauroko. I'd been told it was a challenging route, so before heading to Preservation Inlet, I'd visited the DOC centre in Te Anau to get more detail. The people staffing the front desk had met my request with confused silence, followed by, 'What's the

name of the Great Walk you want a ticket for, sir?' I replied
'Paul's Big Walk Home'. Another silence.

There wasn't much sign of a formed track, although
DOC had marked a basic trail, which was all I needed. I'm
part of a group that looks after abandoned tracks in the
Westland conservancy and our take is that you re-mark
them clearly, but you don't need to go form a new track.
This route was rough and it took a very long day to reach
Hauroko, but it was an interesting walk, through complex
terrain with meandering streams and thick beech forest
ringing with kākā and kākāriki song. At the Albert Burn
and then at the Wairaurāhiri River I crossed using a
'walkwire' – a fancy name for a three-wire swing bridge.

I reached the hut at Teal Bay in afternoon heat. By then,
I'd established a ritual of swimming in all the rivers and
lakes along my route, so I was quickly into the water.
Hauroko is our deepest waterway, and very chilly, but it's
another stunningly beautiful lake.

The hut is a classic from the 1970s, with an open
communal area and two bunkrooms. On the shelves I found
a can of baked beans and one of pineapple. After days of
eating nothing but tramping rations, the humblest canned
food becomes a luxury, and, man, did I enjoy those baked
beans and pineapple slices.

Then it was back into the wilderness and a steep climb
over the tops to Lake Monowai. I had Lake Hauroko below,
and a view of the mountains that I'd come through. That
was an amazing feeling, to see how much country I'd
covered. Much better looking back at what I'd accomplished
than gazing ahead at what was still to come!

I dropped down a bushy spur to Monowai, then worked
my way around the western edge. There was a lot of windfall
around, and the land tended to drop straight to the lake,

with very little shoreline. Eventually, though, I made it to Eel Creek Hut, a tiny but very cosy corrugated-iron A-frame, and got a good fire going.

It was day 11 of my walk home and I allowed myself a bit of a mental pat on the back. I had four more days of tramping before I reached Lake Manapōuri, where I could allow myself a few days of rest in the company of friends. I was looking forward to the next bit, too, because it was going to be all new country. I'd previously travelled the Borland Road, an unsealed 4WD route between Borland Lodge north of Monowai over the Borland Saddle to Lake Manapōuri. This time, I was planning to go cross-country, then climb Mt Titiroa and descend to Manapōuri's south arm.

What stands out from those four days? I remember being inside a little two-bunk hut and hearing the sound of blue duck/whio. When I went outside to look there was a pair of them, along with five juveniles that had just fledged upstream. I also recall feeling a sense of unease contemplating Mt Titiroa, thinking, 'Hell, I have to go over that?!' It turned out to be far more straightforward than it looked. As I went over the top, I spied the farm I was aiming for up the Māraroa River.

The descent from the top of Titiroa was steep and untracked all the way down to the Hope Arm Hut near the shore of Manapōuri. Inside, I found a young Scottish woman on her first overnight visit to a New Zealand backcountry hut. She was probably quite nervous when I turned up, all long beard and wild hair. I went to the lake to have my usual plunge, and found a full can of beer sitting in the shallows. Then back at the hut, I unearthed a couple of tins of mixed fruit that someone had left. The Scot and I shared the beer and fruit that night, and the next morning she walked off reassured that tramping in the backcountry of New Zealand was a safe thing to do.

From the Hope Arm, a well-formed track takes you to the Manapōuri trailhead, but I was determined to walk over untracked country to where the Waiau River joins the Māraroa River, then head up the Māraroa valley.

Generally when I'm crossing large areas of occupied land I find it easier to walk up river valleys than plod along roads. It's quite legal, but where a farm spans both sides of a river, then out of courtesy I like to check in with the landowners. In this case, I'd organised permission to head through five blocks. I made short work of the Māraroa, arriving at my friends' farm at 10.30 pm.

Guy and Lucy Bellerby were a well-known family from the Glenorchy area. Lucy was a horse rider, a keen mountaineer and cross-country skiier. Guy was an old-school high-country mustering type. I'd first met them in the late 1990s on an extended tramping and kayaking trip down south. A friend had told me to give Guy and Lucy a call because he reckoned we'd get on well, and he was right.

Arriving at their farmhouse so late, I was hoping they hadn't all gone to bed. But when I approached the front door, I heard singing. The Bellerbys used to sing together, Mum, Dad and three kids, and on this night they were in full voice. I knocked but no one answered, so I walked inside and through to the lounge. Talk about a surprise visitor. 'Hell, Paul, we weren't expecting you for two more days!' (This is when I first met Lochie, their middle child, then aged 10. We developed an immediate rapport, and shared many laughs and adventures over several years. Sadly Lochie was one of 40 crew members who went missing in the South China Sea when the *Gulf Livestock 1* sank during a typhoon in 2020. I attended his memorial service six months later on the family farm near Manapōuri.)

It was amazing to think I'd walked all the way from Puysegur Point to this valley north of Manapōuri, and I felt a combination of 'I've done it!' and 'Bring on the next bit!' But first I needed a rest. It was three days before Christmas, and I wanted to spend that day with the Bellerbys.

On previous long cross-country trips, I'd posted additional maps and supplies needed for the journey ahead to friends on my route. When I reached their homes, I'd charge up my phone and camera batteries, switch out torches and anything else that needed replacing, and post any letters I'd written along the way. When I got to the Bellerbys' farm, I did just that, restocking my pack with dehydrated meals, some OSM bars and a new set of maps for the country ahead. Meanwhile, Guy, who was pretty well connected in the Otago and South Canterbury farming communities, got on the phone and arranged permission for me to cross a bunch of private properties. (Later, he took a food drop for me to Branches Station near Queenstown, where he was helping with the muster. I'd pick it up many days later, by which time those extra treats were very welcome.)

Christmas day was wonderful. On New Year's Day, we went back to the south coast, to Te Waewae Bay – by vehicle this time – to do some flounder fishing and have a barbecue on the beach. It was perfect weather, and there was not another soul to be seen – until a tourist van turned up and unloaded a Japanese family. With an empty beach to choose from, they sat down next to us. I guess it was a subconscious thing of feeling more comfortable being around people. Anyway, it was nice to share the place with them and attempt some stilted conversation.

That evening, I contemplated what lay ahead. I was about to leave Southland for Otago, followed by the Mackenzie Country. My checklist read: Glenorchy to the Shotover

Valley to the Matukituki and Mt Aspiring National Park, then through to Lake Wānaka, followed by Lake Hāwea, the Ahuriri Valley, Lake Ōhau and Lake Tekapo. It was a lot of rugged and steep country, with few easy stretches. My 'bring-it-on' bravado ebbed for a moment. Was I going to be able to pull this off?

When I left the next morning it was with mixed feelings. Heading off on my own after such a lovely time spent with good people was tough, but I was excited to be back on my journey. I put on my pack, and it felt as familiar as an old friend.

I headed up a tributary called the Whitestone, which originates in the Snowdon Forest north of Te Anau. It was summer and the river was just a trickle, so I walked mostly up a dry gravel bed. At dusk I reached the point where the farmland ended and the bush began, and made camp.

The Snowdon Forest is a handsome piece of beech and tussock country that would have been absolutely stuffed if a hare-brained proposal to build a monorail from Queenstown to Te Anau had gone ahead. I walked from there through to the Mavora Lakes, a pair of serene mountain valley gems, then spent the next few days on the Mavora-Greenstone Walkway, which runs for 50 kilometres between the lakes and the Greenstone Track, much of it in open valley grassland.

Shortly before the Greenstone, I crossed a saddle that marked the border between Southland and Otago. It felt like a significant moment, even if it was just a boggy little clearing in the bush. Guy had told me about a few old musterers' huts that didn't show on the maps, including one well off the track near the saddle that was either Southland's very last hut or Otago's first. I found it and had lunch there, then carried on to the Greenstone Hut.

The hut was packed with trampers, which was a bit of a shock to the system after walking solo. My immediate reaction was to turn around again. I mean, I'd enjoyed that PR aspect of my DOC work, yarning with visitors at huts, but when I'm on a mission it's the last thing I want to do – it's like going back to work! But I got talking to a few people and found myself really enjoying the chat, so I stayed on.

Next morning, I explored a little further up the Greenstone to find a hut that I'd once spied from a distance. It was a private musterers' hut called the Rats' Nest, and I found it near a waterfall. Bagged another one.

There were a couple of side creeks that I was intrigued by, Steele Creek and Kay Creek, that feed from the spectacular Humboldt Mountains north-west of Lake Wakatipu. I decided to follow the former through to Steele Creek Hut, a two-bunk bivvy that was a little run down but would be adequate shelter for a night. As I approached, there was a sudden explosion of noise and limbs – a tiny deer had been sheltering in the doorway and had got such a fright that it had tried to leap into the hut. You hear stories of hunters who struggle for hours to find a deer, and here I was, a mere tramper, practically bumping into one.

From the head of Steele Creek, I dropped down into the Caples Valley to Upper Caples Hut – another crowded one, and muggy with it. There were warnings posted at the hut about slip danger around Kay Creek, but after a cuppa I pushed on to Kay Creek Hut and had no real problems – at least not with the route, which was overgrown in parts but manageable. The hut, however, was a different story. The fine gravel floor had eroded away, leaving rough boulders, and the door was just a piece of wood propped against the opening. The only sleeping area was a piece of black plastic stretched across some boards at one end. I made it cosy enough with my sleeping bag, but then the rain started. As it worsened, water began to creep into the hut between the bunk and fireplace. I lay there thinking, 'At least the roof's solid.' (Since my visit, volunteers have restored the hut to its original state, which I reckon is brilliant – if it had been located in a more accessible part of New Zealand, DOC would have long since demolished it.)

It rained and rained, so I decided to sit the next day out. There was water on the floor, but I had a place to sleep, a fire and plenty of wood to burn. What else did I need? Also, I was reluctant to tackle the next stage in rain because the route ahead didn't look easy.

I have a couple of bibles when it comes to the backcountry, and they're both called 'Moir's'. I had used *Moir's Guide South: The Great Southern Lakes and Fiords* when planning my initial route from Puysegur Point. And now I was using *Moir's Guide North: The Otago Southern Alps* to plot a path through to Wakatipu. (Dr George William Moir was the mountaineer who started the guides back in the 1920s; these days they're updated by a good mate of mine, Geoff Spearpoint, who does a lot of tramping and restoration work on backcountry huts.) I'd also consulted Guy Bellerby, who had experience mustering in the general vicinity, and he'd suggested a route similar to Moir's – over the Humboldt Mountains to Scott Creek and down into the Routeburn Valley.

Looking from Kay Creek towards the Humboldts it appeared to be steep and rugged. But when the rain finally stopped and I was into my stride again, I realised I shouldn't have worried. In fact, it was fairly easy walking, zig-zagging up through tussockland and among big boulders, up to some nice plateau country, with no need for any death-defying climbing. It's a familiar story: when you look at steep mountain country from a distance it always seems daunting, but once you're up close the route reveals itself. In this case, musterers had once pushed sheep through the Humboldts, and where sheep can go a human can.

From the tops you could see a tussock basin where the beech forest started, and the head of Scott Creek. When I got down to the bush edge, I found a historic stock track. It was overgrown and there was a fair bit of windfall scattered around, but it was substantial enough and I followed it all the way through to the Dart Valley.

Cue the appearance of a highway. Rather than follow it to Glenorchy, I stuck to the Dart riverbed, the river still low despite the rain. It was a pleasant, meandering route through semi-wilderness and the only thing that shattered my peace was a tourist jet boat, which came close so the passengers could wave to me. I waved back, nice and friendly, while they filmed. I was a 'New Zealander in the Wild', or perhaps 'New Zealand Wildlife'. On reflection, it was probably the latter.

I'd expected to have to do a serious stock-up at Glenorchy, but I had plenty of food left in my pack. It seems like the more I walk, the less I need to eat. Part of that is probably down to my emotional state on these longer tramps. I'm feeling good, the air's fresh and I'm under no pressure to be anywhere at any particular time. So I'm totally relaxed, and my metabolism or something changes as a result. It makes me wonder whether in normal life, with all its stress, we overcompensate by eating more than we need. In any case, my food was lasting longer and longer. Sure I had dropped a bit of weight – by the time I hit Tekapo I'd lost eight kilograms – but I was feeling content and full of energy.

In Glenorchy, where I stayed three nights in a camping-ground cabin, some nice people invited me out for a meal at the pub. They must have said something to the cook, because he came out and said to me, 'You're the fella doing the big walk, right?', then desposited two fat steaks and a small mountain of spuds on my plate. I got a doggie bag, and I was still eating from it three days later.

From Glenorchy, I was targeting The Branches, one of New Zealand's most isolated high-country stations. It's a magnificent 30,000-hectare property, set between the Richardson Range to the west and the Harris Range to the east, with its head rubbing against Mt Aspiring National Park. To reach the station by vehicle from Queenstown you have to brave the length of the legendary Skippers Road, a narrow, slip-prone 4WD route set dizzingly high above Skippers Canyon. I was coming from the west, over the Richardsons. I'd talked to Guy, who'd mustered those same mountains many times, but my plan was sketchy. I'd have to work it out as I went along.

*

In the Whakaari Conservation Area, on the western faces above Glenorchy, I encountered a series of old huts with evocative names – Mt Judah, Heather Jock, Bonnie Jean – built by early scheelite miners using corrugated iron, weathered bits of timber and stone for the floors. They were relics of a history that few people know, a kind of sidebar to the gold rushes. Scheelite, which is used to produce tungsten, was discovered near Glenorchy in the 1880s, and for a while it fetched a pretty penny. But the miners had to work hard for their money, carving tunnels deep into the mountains and digging out the scheelite-bearing quartz by hand. Apart from the huts, they'd left behind other relics, including the remains of a cableway used to transport diggings across gullies, and a shed with an ancient Nuffield tractor parked inside. After having to climb like a mountain goat to reach the place, I couldn't believe that they'd actually got a tractor up there.

Most of the huts had been restored and were now maintained pretty much as museum pieces, but you could stay overnight at the Heather Jock Hut. It was one of the more spectacularly sited of them at 1400 metres in steep tussock country, with views back towards the head of Lake Wakatipu and beyond to the mountains of the Caples and Greenstone.

From there I followed an old miners' track to Larkins Slip Hut, which was all but falling over and not long for this world, then down to Wallers Hut. Built in the 1920s using corrugated iron and beech sourced from the neighbouring forest, Wallers had also seen better days. Happily, it was comprehensively restored soon after my visit and, I believe, is still offering shelter to hill-weary trampers.

By Wallers Hut, my knowledge of the route ahead was almost exhausted. I spent an afternoon scouting out my next move, then went for it, climbing up a steepish bushy slope that led to open tussockland, then into snow country. I traversed under a series of large bluffs, but now a mist had descended and my visibility was almost gone. I consulted the map for guidance, aware as I did that the contour lines were spaced 20 metres apart. A lot can go wrong in 20 metres!

I came upon a high bluff wall. Below it a steep, snow-covered scree slope disappeared into the mist. 'Bugger this,' I thought, and headed down, working hard to keep my feet until I reached plateau country. I found out later it was the same saddle that kids from Glenorchy used to walk over to reach Skippers School at the start of every week.

I crossed over the saddle near the Wallers Creek headwaters, with a view down into a tributary of Stoney

Creek. My God, it was steep – close enough to vertical. As cloud cleared, I spotted a far safer route, and took it down through beech forest to Shed Creek, which flowed into Stoney Creek.

As I approached the little two-bunk hut near the creek I could see smoke rising from the chimney, and a heavy cloud of tobacco smoke exiting the door. There was a scattering of empty beer cans outside, along with a drying tent fly and what looked to be mining gear. A voice said, 'Gidday, mate, how're you doing?', and that's how I met Dave Greenslade.

Yeats Ridge Hut, Hokitika area.

Chapter 24

Dave was what I guess you'd call a character. I've met a few. Swaggers. Prospectors. Bush pilots. Backcountry hermits.

I once filled out a form that needed to be witnessed by a 'reputable person'. I thought, 'In my opinion all of my friends are reputable persons.' It's the same with the word 'character'. What's a character? Is it a matter of eccentricity? Of being an outsider? In any case, on my wanderings I've met plenty of characters who fascinated me. Some I met in passing; others I got to know pretty well.

The late Westie – Owen West – of Westies Hut fame was one of the best. I met him many years ago on a trip to Big River. Westie was born and bred in Bluff of southern Māori heritage, a commercial fisherman who knew that coastline intimately. He was solid, with muscular legs and strong arms, long hair that he usually kept in a ponytail and a bushy beard framing a massive, winning smile.

He was generous – the first time I met him he offered me the use of his camp while he was away – and he was deceptively gentle. Once, he was hunting a hind when it turned and looked at him, staring hard into his eyes. After that, he never killed another deer! He liked baking scones and writing letters. People would send mail to 'Westie at Prices Harbour, South Coast Track, New Zealand' and it would find its way to an Invercargill address he was connected to, and eventually on to him.

But Westie took no bullshit. Witness the story of how he came to be living in a sea cave on the southern coast. In 1986 he was serving as the mandatory Kiwi skipper on an Aussie-owned commercial fishing boat in those waters when he got into a bitter row with the seven-man Aussie crew. Eventually, he told them to get stuffed, jumped overboard, swam to shore, then made his way around the coast to Prices Harbour where he'd heard of a rudimentary cave shelter. He camped there for eight years, living off the land.

I only once saw Westie's steely side. It was the last time I met him, at the Waitutu Hut. I'd just arrived and he was already there. We had a good catch-up and had just shared dinner when a helicopter arrived with six Southland hunters. The first thing they did was open their whisky and get pissed out of their brains. One went outside with his rifle and starting shooting. Westie got volcanically angry about that, gave them a massive bollocking, and then lit up a fat joint. Now, I don't smoke, but I enjoyed this show. One of these guys blustered, 'You're using a drug!' Westie and I pissed ourselves laughing about that.

Dope was Westie's tipple – his hut book was decorated with a hand-drawn marijuana leaf, and he smoked every day. Fifteen cops in two Iroquois choppers once descended on his camp because they'd heard a rumour that he was a major grower – as Westie said, there were so many possums down there you'd never have made a dime, but the police thought they knew better. When they landed on the beach, he asked if they wanted to see his dope, then showed them three scrawny plants out back. Before they left he badgered those drug cops to sign his visitor book!

Contrary to appearances, Westie wasn't a hermit. Periodically, he'd stay in a cabin at the Tūātapere camping ground, chatting with the residents and writing letters to people all around the world – myself included. But there's no denying he had his eccentricities. He sluiced for gold in Big River wearing studded rugby boots. He lined his hut with wallpaper to keep out the draughts. When he wanted a lift, he'd hang out a banner painted with 'TAXI' for a friendly chopper pilot to spot. God, he was a good man.

*

Tom Ryan was from a well-known Stewart Island Māori family. I met him in early 1974 while tramping around the island – my first time on Rakiura. Two of the people in our group were racehorses, while me and a friend brought up the rear. It was the 'Tail-end Charlies' who smelled the smoke while walking down East Ruggedy Beach. There wasn't supposed to be a hut there, but we followed our noses and found one. We were warmly greeted by Tom, who invited us in for a cuppa. He told us that this was traditional Māori land and that he'd made it his home since his wife died years earlier. His one-bedroom hut was the size of a standard six-bunk Forest Service hut, built from old iron and bits of salvaged timber, with a brick fireplace and rocks stacked up to the sill to break the wind.

Tom was a hunter and fisherman, grew his own veges and had planted several fruit trees. He kept rows and rows of bottled peaches and plums, as well as big drums full of salted briny water in which he kept his venison. There was a pathway to a little cove nearby where a boat could beach on high tide. He seemed very happy with his lot. What happened to him I don't know, but ten years ago I did some work for DOC near

East Ruggedy Beach and searched for his hut – there was nothing left of it but a handful of foundation posts.

Tom's nearest neighbour – as in three or four days' walk away – was Tim Te Aika's family at Island Hill Station, one of New Zealand's most remote farms. I met Tim on that same trip, had a cuppa on his porch while his 'pet' kiwi hovered nearby. (On Stewart Island, kiwi tend to wander around during the day, and this character was particularly friendly.) Tim had tried all sorts of things to make a living in that remote place. In the nearby sand you could see the remains of a tractor he'd used to ship wool bales from the beach. Later he'd decided that flying the wool out might be easier, so he'd got his pilot's licence and built an airstrip.

When I met those two guys, Tom and Tim, I felt envious of their remote circumstances. I was still in my twenties, and didn't yet grasp just how important social connections are. To see someone like Tom happily alone, breathing in fresh air, having silence and solitude when he wanted it, appealed hugely to me.

*

In 1972, a group of us from the Marlborough Tramping Club were walking the Wangapeka Track near Nelson and arrived at King's Hut. There was a note on the door that said: 'If you've just stopped for a cup of tea, walk a few minutes more, the billy is always boiling at my hut.' And so we met gold prospector Cecil King. He didn't live in his hut full-time – just four months of the year, I think, and the rest in Wellington – but he would always be pining to get back to the Wangapeka. He was another guy who was totally content pottering away in the backcountry.

A friend of mine met Cecil on another occasion. He told me how he went to the hut and yelled hello, and heard a response from behind. He investigated and found a great big hole, with a fella at the bottom digging furiously – Cecil. He asked him if he'd found any gold, and Cecil replied, 'Nah, only fly shit,' then threw up a jar full of gold dust. My mate said, 'If that's what he calls fly shit, I'd love to see what his version of gold looks like.'

*

Peter and Valerie Bell were farmers up the Wangapeka who also served as rangers. They lived in a farmhouse beside the road, which was where you checked in before you headed into the hills. If they were home they'd always offer a cuppa; if they weren't, then you just walked in and signed the book.

They had impeccable bush knowledge, and would squeeze you for details about track conditions. Years later I arrived at a hut in the Mt Arthur tablelands and saw an old fella sitting by himself – it was Peter. He was in his eighties by then, but still tramping. We talked about the surrounding country and even there, far away from his beloved Wangapeka Valley, he had a strong and in-depth knowledge of his surroundings.

*

Robert Long (aka 'Beansprout') and his wife Catherine live in a hut at Gorge River, South Westland. In Robert's case, he's been there since he dropped out of medical school in 1980. I met them twice while tramping in the area, and once I flew down to see them. There's an airstrip near the hut that they keep well maintained.

Robert found the hut in 1979. It was a basic two-room shack that had been abandoned, but he tracked down the owner, a whitebaiter who had jet boats and airplanes and a crayfishing business, but who hadn't been able to make the economics work from the location. They reached a gentleman's agreement that Robert could stay in the hut and have rights to its use for as long as he wished. So he did just that. He was an expat Aussie, looking for somewhere off the beaten track where he could live closer to nature. Over time, he rebuilt the hut one section at a time, and it's strong and solid now, and very homely.

Still, it's an incredibly isolated spot. If they were to walk north, they could probably reach the end of Jackson Bay Road in two to three days; head south and they could get through the Hollyford Valley to civilisation in six. Mostly, they fly. They raised two kids there, with just a monthly airborne resupply, plus a couple of trips into the outside world per year. When Robert wrote his memoir *A Life on Gorge River*, he subtitled it 'New Zealand's Remotest Family'.

When you live in such a lonely location and your health starts to go, it would quickly become a pretty tough life, I imagine. Beansprout and Catherine are well aware there'll come a time when they have to move somewhere less isolated. But for now they seem happy and secure there, living off the land. They do a lot of fishing and the odd bit of trapping. Robert paints, too, and sells his work on commission. Again, they're people who appear to be living like hermits, but they're actually extremely social, highly intelligent and have lots of friends who visit.

*

On the old inch-to-mile maps of the Upper Tākaka to Mt Arthur Tableland pack track there's a spot at Barren Flat marked 'Snowy's Hut'. It's a reference to Snow Myers, aka the 'Hermit of the Bend', who lived in that hut on the site of an abandoned mill for 15 years.

Although he liked to tell everyone it was his place, Snow was the ultimate hut squatter. When the land around it was bought by ex-forest ranger Piers Maclaren in 1974, Snow very reluctantly moved on. He ended up squatting at Leslie Clearing Hut, a short distance up the valley from the Karamea Bend in the Kahurangi National Park. Later he lived at Luna Hut in the upper reaches of the Karamea River not far from the Wangapeka Track, where he became a sort of honorary ranger. He wore a ranger's shirt, did ranger work, and offered advice to hunters and trampers.

Snow had heart surgery at Greenlane Hospital at the same time that my father, Bob, was there. Years later, on a tramp, I called in at the Leslie Clearing Hut and met Snow for the first time. I said, 'Gidday, I'm Paul Kilgour.'

'Any relation to Bob?'

'Yep, his son.'

'Oh, mate, Bob was a good bugger. Gee, this calls for a celebration – the son of Bob!'

Snow put on some camp-oven bread, then we went down to the river where he caught a very large trout. It was a terrific meal, and a highly entertaining evening.

Snow later moved into a hut on a friend's farm up the Motueka Valley, where he died suddenly of a massive heart attack. Luna Hut was shifted to a covenanted piece of land near Tapawera and you can make arrangements to look at it. It's just as it was when it was on the Karamea River, right down to the graffiti on the wall.

*

While hitching overseas I met some terrific characters. I was only in their company for a brief time, but they made an unforgettable impression. In Scotland, I was hitching north of Inverness when a little Morrie 1000 came screeching to a halt beside me. Inside was a big fella in full Scottish clan regalia, the kilt, hat and sporran. I climbed in and tried to make friendly conversation, but didn't get much response beyond a few grudging grunts. Then, out of the blue, he started talking.

'Lad, this is a terrible day,' he said.

'Why's that?'

'Because I'm a Scotsman and I'm wasting my time and my money.'

'I'm sorry to hear that. What's the problem?'

'I've got to make this damned trip to town.'

'Why?'

'I need a new comb.' He lifted his hat. He was practically bald.

'Why?'

'I've broken a tooth on my old comb.'

'But you can still use a comb with a broken tooth.'

Without missing a beat he said, 'Ah but laddie, it was the last tooth.' He carried on driving. To this day I'm not sure if he was having me on.

Also in Scotland, I once got a lift from a judge. He seemed friendly enough, but I thought, 'He's a judge; I'll mind what I say.'

There's that old line about how you can't judge a book by its cover. Well, in this case you couldn't judge a judge. As soon as he heard I was from New Zealand, he started raving about our Nuclear Free policy. Then he started quizzing me about organic gardening in New Zealand. Eventually we arrived at his home, a beautiful and historic stone cottage down a long country lane. The entrance was a traditional archway, but it had been painted with a rainbow and the words 'Nuclear Free Zone'. I thought, 'That confirms it: this judge is different!'

A fat and friendly Labrador came up to greet me. In its mouth was a rubber squishy toy that squeaked every time the dog bit down. I looked more closely and saw it was a Margaret Thatcher doll. The judge was quietly, via his canine, expressing his view of the Iron Lady. After lunch he put on his golfing gear, drove me a few more miles down the road to his club and waved goodbye.

*

So there I was at Stoney Creek Hut, on the cusp of adding another backcountry character to the pantheon. Dave Greenslade was from Haast and a latter-day gold prospector. How long had he been in the hills near Queenstown? Dave either didn't know or wouldn't tell me. With some backcountry people, time just doesn't strike them as important. I remember chatting with an old fella in Tennessee once, and I said something like 'You been here all your life?' He replied, 'Not yet, son, not yet.' However long Dave had been prospecting, he'd clearly had some success. When I once asked someone from Haast if they knew Dave Greenslade, they said, 'Oh, that wealthy bastard! He's just bought himself another house!'

Dave was rough as guts at first glance — the beer cans scattered outside the hut were a sign — but a teddy bear on the inside. After a bit of banter, he invited me to stay the night, telling me that he was just back from the supermarket and had enough food to feed a tribe. When I expressed some doubt – the supermarket, really? – he explained. 'See that spot over there?' he said, pointing to a grassy flat. 'I go out there and call the Queenstown heli company with my satellite phone and they're here in a flash. They fly me to their base at Frankton, just across the carpark from the supermarket; I wheel out a couple of trolleys full of food back to the chopper, and they fly me back. I'm barely gone an hour.'

That night in the remote hills we feasted on roast potatoes and mutton stew, cooked on a camp oven, followed by dessert with fresh cream. The following morning it was bacon and eggs, washed down with strong coffee.

After breakfast, Dave showed me a route to Skippers and gave me some notes to drop to his friends along the way – they were written on a crinkly piece of paper like an old treasure map, which seemed apt for Dave. He also made me a classic musterer's hill stick, using a sapling with a rounded head and a point at the other end. You can use these sticks for support when you're traversing a slope, planting them uphill and leaning in, or for crossing a fast-flowing stream or river. They're pretty handy for fending off bird attacks, too. Once, when I inflamed a mother falcon by getting too close to her nest, I stuck my hat on the end of my hill stick as a dummy – she went after it hard! The stick Dave made for me was so strong that I was able to use it to lower myself down between rocks, pack and all.

Westies Hut, on my traverse home, December 2007.

Chapter 25

By the end of that day, I'd reached Skippers and crossed the bridge and was well on my way up the road into The Branches. It might as well have been a backcountry track it was so lonely. At one point I passed a burned-out car, which was a bit spooky, but I saw and heard nobody.

It was seriously raw country, and while the day was pleasant enough, you could tell that it would be an extreme environment to live in, sunless and bitterly cold in winter, and blazingly hot and exposed in high summer. As I walked, I thought about the human history of the place, particularly those early miners who swarmed into the gorge's upper reaches after gold. I've always been fascinated by how landscape moulds people, how it can make or break you. What kind of character would you have needed to endure a place like Skippers in the 1860s?

There were some old huts along the route and, naturally, I checked them out. In one, I found a note for me! It was from Guy, telling me the names of the people at Branches Station and that they were expecting me at the manager's house. When I eventually met the manager and his family, they had another treasure hunt-type note from Guy letting me know where my food drop was. It was along the lines of 'Go to the old shearers' quarters; find room four; your food will be on the second bunk on the right'. When I got there, I discovered that someone had added a heap of chocolate, fruit and beer to the pile. These anonymous acts of kindness kept happening on my big walk home, and were always welcome.

I had a belly-filling lunch with the manager's family. It's always funny how, when you get to a backcountry farm, the bloke tends to say, 'Mate, you look like you need a good feed of greasy chops,' and the woman will say, 'Poor love, you could do with a nice salad and some fresh fruit!' For me, it was all good. I certainly didn't worry about how fattening the food was – I'd soon burn it off!

Branches Station was a beautiful farm, and it came with a mystery. Years earlier, owner and backcountry legend Arthur Borrell had disappeared while walking the property. A note was found in one of the mustering huts saying that he was off to photograph some snowgrass tussock. Eventually, a search party located his shirt and shorts in the Shiel Burn River. Arthur often went barefoot, and it was speculated he may have slipped and fallen into the water, but no other sign of him was ever found.

I stayed a night at the same Shiel Burn Hut, then left my gear at 100 Mile Hut and backtracked to Lochnagar. This little lake in a bowl of high peaks had captured my imagination when I saw it on a map, and I'd wanted to visit it ever since. It was worth the wait, a genuine alpine stunner, and as a bonus I bagged my 900th backcountry hut on its shores. Lochnagar Hut had been built by Arthur Borrell from mining-era relics and other salvaged bits and pieces, which gave it a quirky character. Its chimney was made from a steel drainpipe stitched together with clunky rivets, it had a recycled window set in the doorway, and the roof was so low you had to stoop hard to get in, but it was snug and comfortable. Just as well, because I was just settling in when it began to rain heavily. That night I read all the old entries in the hut book, including a few zingers from Arthur. He sure hated bureaucrats telling him how to run his farm!

After retrieving my gear the next morning, I made my way to the head of the Shotover and Tummel Burn Hut (memorable primarily for having a roof so low you couldn't stand upright) where I rested up before attempting the next day's slog to the Shotover Saddle. I had heard it wasn't the easiest route, with thick scrub and some sheer bluffs that were best avoided, and the entries in the Tummel Burn hut book confirmed it. Along with a write-up from a mad Canadian who'd carted his mountain bike up there in parts, there were accounts of people getting themselves horribly lost coming from the other end.

When you read reports of other trampers' ordeals, it gives you pause – but not in a bad way. It tends to make me stand back and really nut out my route. How would a person logically do this? What does the terrain and vegetation suggest? As long as I'm not rushed, I can generally figure out a viable path through a piece of tough country. Occasionally you'll come across a rock cairn or other marker that shows you're on track; or you might find the high-country vegetation is thicker than expected, which can force a rethink. You work your way around such obstacles, and get there in the end – at least, that's been my experience.

When I finally reached the Shotover Saddle and took a breather, I had a lovely experience with about a dozen kea keeping me company. There was one kea on my boot, another on my pack, and one actually standing on my back – kea everywhere you looked. It was a lovely payoff for what had been a hard slog.

The Shotover Saddle is at the head of a river system that flows southwards. From my rest stop, I looked directly down into the Matukituki Valley, which runs at right angles to the saddle, taking cautious note of the steepness of the slope to the valley floor. The saddle is the dividing point between the valleys of South and Central Otago, and from this high point the contrast in terrain was striking. But the landform that kept snagging my attention was the Matterhorn-like peak of Tititea/Mt Aspiring. I found it beautiful but melancholy: years earlier, my good mate and kayaking buddy Gavin Cedarman had fallen to his death up there. I've seen the footage he took right up until moments before he fell, and he was clearly enjoying himself, so I guess you just have to celebrate that.

After carefully picking my way down to the Matukituki Valley, I spent that night at Aspiring Hut, sharing it with a DOC hut warden and an English couple. We had one of those funny two-degrees-of-separation moments. When I said I was from Golden Bay, they told me there was a woman living near Nelson whom they wanted to reach. Problem was they didn't have her details. Me: 'What's her name?' 'Sue Something-or-other.' 'Sue! Oh, I know Sue. Actually, I've got her phone number!' She's a former girlfriend.

The hut warden was due to radio her HQ, and asked if I wanted to get a message to anyone. I told her that I had friends at Makarora, Bruce and Jeanette Gillies, who were my safety people for this part of the journey. Could she let them know that I was heading on to Albert Burn, then across to the head of Lake Wānaka, before catching up with them for a night or two? There was a big storm forecast, so they weren't to panic if I didn't make my deadline; I'd be holed up somewhere, most likely at the Albert Burn Hut. It proved to be a timely warning.

I left early the next morning, but by the time I reached the Raspberry Creek carpark at the head of the track I'd greeted at least 80 walkers heading the other way. That walk has become hugely popular with tourists, and you could smell the perfume of the city on them. I still remember tramping that same valley in the 1970s when there was no carpark, when you had to leave your vehicle on the side of the road and pray that the keas didn't find it.

I've previously mentioned a meteor shower I once saw in the Matukituki Valley, and it was on my mind now as I traversed from the west to the east branch. Looking up the valley, I thought I saw the spot where we must have camped, and tried to bring back that scene. There was a strong sense of completing a circle. Shooting stars above the Matukituki had felt like a sign validating my wandering lifestyle, and now I was back on my most ambitious and challenging walk to date.

The next days were memorable for particularly spine-tingling swing-bridge crossings – including two in memory of ecologist and alpine explorer Jack Holloway – as well as some hairy moments sidling around steep bluffs and gorges as I worked my way from the Matukituki River East Branch to the Albert Burn Valley. The hill stick that Dave Greenslade had made me now came into its own. At one point, I even used it to lower myself down a near-vertical face – bless you, Dave!

At the Albert Burn Saddle, I paused for a long moment to take stock. Aspiring lay to the west, closer than when I'd seen it from the Shotover Saddle, and to the north I caught a glimpse of Aoraki/Mt Cook. It was a milestone on my walk, and I had a powerful sense of achievement. I thought, 'I can see where I've been; I can see where I'm heading; and I'm enjoying where I am.' The other thing I realised was how quickly I'd covered seemingly vast distances without even really pushing myself. It was a reminder of how efficient walking can be. I was just plodding along, without any firm deadline, not letting myself race towards a goal, and yet I was burning through the miles.

The Albert Burn Hut was a standard six-bunker built in the 1990s to replace a Forest Service original that had burned down, with a wood stove and a nice big verandah and roomy platform bunks of which I could take my pick – I had the hut to myself. Happily, the cupboards were full of food that hunters had left behind, the likes of tinned corned beef, baked beans and even some eggs, and the hut was well positioned on a terrace some distance from the river. As it turned out, it was the perfect place to hunker down in terrible weather.

I felt the storm long before the rain started, an atmospheric signal that something was about to unleash. The morning had been warm, and by mid-afternoon it had clouded over and become even hotter. It was still and silent – even the birds had gone quiet. I gathered as much firewood as possible, had a good wash under a little waterfall (I have 'before and after' photos of those falls pre- and post-rainfall and the contrast in water flow is incredible) and got a meal ready. An hour or so before dark, the skies opened and unleashed a terrific hammering on the hut's tin roof.

What I remember is how explosively the storm began and the sheer volume of water. By the time the sun went down, the river was already running high. For the next day and night and into a third day, it didn't relent. By the end, the little waterfall I'd bathed in had grown thunderously loud, and from the hut you could also hear the thumping of rocks, logs and even entire trees in the frothing cauldron of the Albert Burn. It didn't take me long to realise that heading downriver was impossible and that the hut was a good place to be – even if it meant I'd be overdue at Makarora.

(I heard later that during the same storm, a group of four trampers from Nelson left a perfectly good hut at Kerrin Forks and headed down the true right of the Wilkin River.

When they realised the futility of it, they turned back, but were then cut off by a swollen side creek and spent a miserable time huddled under a tent fly.)

With ingredients I found in the cupboards, I made date scones, and drizzled on leftover maple syrup. It wasn't really such a hardship to be stranded! I wrote letters – lots of them. On a big trip like mine, you welcome any excuse to stop. Also, I was savouring the power of the elements – in a strange way, I was being energised by the deluge.

Eventually, the rain eased and the river finally started to drop. I left the hut on the third morning. Later, I learned that my friends in Makarora had a posse primed to go looking for me the following day if I hadn't shown, with a Unimog 4WD to cross the streams and a chopper lined up. No one was panicking, but they were watching out for me all the same.

Heading down the valley, I still had to do a couple of chest-high river crossings – once again, Dave's hill stick came in handy – before reaching the edge of Lake Wānaka. There I picked up an overgrown stock track, and followed it for a couple of hours to an old hut near where the Makarora River flowed in at the head of the lake.

The Craigie Burn Hut was a former homestead that had seen far better days. When I saw the nearby Makarora flowing high and fast, spewing logs and mud and slurry, my heart sank. I thought, 'Am I really going to have to wait it out in this place?' My eyes fell on a scrap of yellow paper tucked under a rock. To my huge surprise, it was a note from my Makarora friends. It said: 'Paul, when you get here, hang this orange sack in the tree outside where we can see it from the bach.' Within an hour I heard a jet boat start on the far side of the lake, and soon after saw Bruce and Jeanette and their dog Katie approaching. In the excitement of boarding the boat, I left the hill stick behind, but it didn't go to waste: whenever Bruce passes by Craigie Burn on hunting trips he makes a point of grabbing it to use.

*

Makarora township is just up the valley from the top of Lake Wānaka. It's a tight little community, with a sprinkling of permanent residents, retired people with baches, seasonal workers and farmers. The night I arrived was the annual Makarora barbecue, and when we turned up it almost felt like I was the guest of honour. There was the local DOC and SAR person, the area cop, pilots and landowners, all keen to know how I'd weathered the storm.

Among the people I met that night was the manager of Mt Albert Station, who was involved with the Swazi outdoor clothing company. Not only did he test their gear while working on the farm, he features in Swazi brochures, including one I'd always found amusing. It shows a bloke completely naked in a mountain valley, and the slogan 'It's Swazi or it's nothing!'. I said to him, 'Hello, I think I've seen your picture, but it's hard to recognise you in clothes.'

I was also introduced to a local helicopter pilot, Harvey Hutton, who was taking his machine to Wānaka the next day for servicing and offered me a lift to do my shopping. We had a terrific low-level flight through the mountains between Hāwea and Wānaka, and later while stocking up at the supermarket I bumped into an old friend, Heather White, who I went to primary school with at Waimauku (daughter of Max White, ex Tōtaranui park ranger). We Kiwis get a bit blasé about these chance meetings, but I always find it a thrill, especially after you've been alone in the hills for a few weeks.

I had three nights in Makarora, sleeping in a soft bed

with fresh sheets. On the fourth day, Bruce dropped me off at Cameron Creek and I started walking again in earnest.

Cameron Creek flows out of the mountains east of Makarora. From the head, you can get into the Hunter Valley via the Highburn Creek, but it is very gorgy country. In 1983, I'd got myself hugely bluffed in the area, and been forced to backtrack for an hour. I'd since learned that there was a stock track winding up through the bluffs and this time I took it. It was narrow and steep, but I figured that if cattle used it then so could I. That optimism was challenged as I started to come across dead animals, all shot in the head where they'd fallen off bluffs and broken their legs.

From the Highburn Valley I headed down to the Hunter River, where I spotted two horses heading my way. It turned out to be the station manager's wife and daughter. We boiled the billy at a nearby hut and had a cuppa while the daughter warned me about some of the hazards of crossing around the head of Lake Hāwea. They included quicksand, soft lake edges and deep swamps where they periodically lost animals, but using my map she showed me a good way through. I really appreciated the last-minute insider's advice.

On the other side of Hāwea, I found a newly built mountain-bike track and followed it down through patches of beech forest to a lakeside campsite for the night, then on to the Dingle Burn Valley.

Coming around a corner, I saw a guy fishing. He took one look at me and said, 'Are you Paul Kilgour?' I confirmed. 'Well, Aarn Tate says gidday.'

Aarn Tate is the man who developed the 'balance' packs that I'm such a fan of. They have an ingenious harness system with big front pockets, which brings the centre of gravity forward so you keep your back vertical rather than constantly leaning forward. In my fifties, I developed back problems and was told I'd never be able to carry a pack again. I got an Aarn pack and it saved my tramping career.

The fisherman said he worked with Aarn on pack development, and reached for his satellite phone. 'Hey Aarn, I've just met a fine fellow with a fine pack doing a fine traverse.' Aarn said, 'Is it Paul? Put him on.'

My pack had taken quite a few knocks, and I'd had to replace bits along the way. The repairs were all very makeshift – a piece of hardwood here, parts of a scavenged bike derailleur there. Aarn asked where I was planning to stop next for a rest and I told him Twizel. Days later when I reached Twizel, Aarn had couriered an envelope so I could send him my pack for a complete repair. He did it in two days, patching holes, replacing straps and fitting a complete new harness system. Now that's excellent product follow-up – and by the company's CEO, no less!

My new fisherman friend was heading out to the road, but he walked with me as far as the next hut and prepared a trout for our lunch. Man, it was beautiful. He even had a bit of lemon to squeeze on.

I wanted to explore as much new country as possible, and was keen to get over to the Timaru River, which flows into Lake Hāwea. From there I'd head northwards into the Avon Burn, which in turn would get me into the Ahuriri Valley at the southern end of the Mackenzie Country. I started cross-country, then slowly made my way up through beech forest on the south face of the Dingle Burn. Near the bush edge I found the Mae West Bivouac. I'd read in my guidebook that it was a two-bunk bivvy. In fact, it was a corrugated-iron seven-bunk hut that had once been part of Dingleburn Station but was now being swamped by beech regrowth. It had sapling-and-sacking bunks, a rough gravel floor and had definitely seen better days. I decided not to put its questionable comforts to the test, and instead climbed up to a low saddle and on to the Top Timaru Hut, a newish six-bunker on the Te Araroa Trail. It took me another three hours over a false saddle before I got there.

The next day I followed an overgrown 4WD farm track over a high saddle, through rolling tussockland into vast scree country, then into the tributaries of the Avon Burn and down to the Ahuriri Valley. It was all private farmland, but before I left Golden Bay I'd arranged permission from the owner, Jim Morris, to cross. Jim is a big, gruff high-country farmer. When I asked him if I could walk through his station, he barked, 'Yep, but on one condition!' 'What?' 'You have to come to the homestead for some high-country hospitality. Have we got a deal?'

After making my way down the Ben Avon tributaries, I found a fenceline and made a beeline for the homestead. Jim proved as good as his word, and we spent several hours chatting over a big country lunch and cups of tea.

Eventually, I excused myself to make a call home, my first since Makarora. It was a difficult conversation. Janet had just returned from Antartica, where she'd had a job at a remote field camp that catered for wealthy (and demanding) adventure tourists. The job hadn't matched the description, and she'd returned burnt-out and depressed. She was struggling, and I said I'd come home.

I had mixed feelings, but it was the right thing to do. As well, I was starting to realise that even though I was in dry country, the rivers were far higher than normal and becoming challenging to cross. I'd lost eight kilos — you could have played a tune on my ribcage — and while I was feeling fit and healthy, I'd started to look forward to getting to bed every day, and sleeping longer and deeper. I decided I'd continue as far as Tekapo, then head immediately to Golden Bay.

After getting some advice from Jim, I found a good place to cross the Ahuriri River and walked on to Hideaway Hut near Camp Creek. It's one of our oldest backcountry huts, built in the nineteenth century for musterers from Benmore Station, an absolutely massive sheep run that included the Ahuriri Valley and a fair whack of the Mackenzie Country. The hut, by contrast, was tiny, just two bunks, with beech-pole walls and roof framing covered in corrugated iron. Some of the earliest musterers' names are pencilled on the tin exterior, including one dating from 1895.

From there, I moved quickly from Snowy Gorge Creek and Snowy Gorge Hut, over the Maitland Saddle and down to the Maitland Stream, then via a farm track to Lake Ōhau Station and across country to the Lake Ōhau outlet. Over the next three days, I connected the dots to Twizel, to Pūkaki, to Tekapo, walking alongside those brilliantly blue canals that stretch across the Mackenzie.

It was hot and I was walking most days in a mouth-drying wind. The contrast with where I'd started my walk couldn't have been starker. From dripping-wet Fiordland bush to an arid basin under a big sky. And I knew that not so far away as the crow flies was lush West Coast rainforest, which is different again. You notice those transitions when you're driving – say, when you drive through Arthur's Pass from the West Coast to Canterbury – but when you do it on foot it seems so much more abrupt. You step out from the last bit of bush in the Dingle Burn, and then you're over a saddle and there's no more bush for a very long way.

I sheltered behind a hill for a while and watched tussock dancing in the wind, a harrier hawk circling above. It was every bit as beautiful as anything I'd seen so far. I was appalled, though, at the number of rabbit holes and the obvious impact of vermin. I remembered an earlier time when I was driving up the side of Lake Tekapo and came around a corner to see a wild cat with a native bird in its mouth. It went straight under my wheels – clunk, clunk. Days later when I drove back the other way, there was a ferret on the road feeding on the cat roadkill. It looked up, too late – clunk. I thought, 'That's a double score for conservation.'

When I got to Tekapo, I wanted to strip and plunge into the lake, but there was a busload of tourists on the shore. I left my clothes on and jumped in anyway. I had a right to celebrate. I'd walked 45 days from Puysegur Point, and covered a distance of 854 kilometres. I was tired, sure, but I was super fit and would have loved to have kept going. I had a strong feeling of 'I must come back and finish this'.

I know that people who walk the Te Araroa Trail have different philosophies about this kind of thing. Some will accept a lift on the road; others would rather cut their thumb off. They are the 'EFIs', the Every Fucking Inch types. Me? I'd set myself a challenge and now I was changing the rules. Was I cheating? I thought, 'I'm still going to walk home; I'm just breaking it in half.' Some people will say, 'Yes, but you did it in two sections.' My response: it was my adventure, my rules.

A friend who was driving through to Christchurch picked me up. I stayed the night in a cabin near Christchurch Airport and arrived at the terminal the next day just as a hostage drama was playing out. The terminal was locked down and a large crowd was milling outside. It was a rude awakening after the peace and solitude of the previous 45 days.

Back in Golden Bay, I was able to be supportive for Janet – a different kind of challenge. Life carried on. I went to Australia to see my daughter and first grandson. But at the back of my mind, there was a feeling of unfinished business. When the timing was right, I'd pick up the trail again.

Lake Hankinson Hut, Fiordland, George Sound Track, April 1999.

Chapter 26

To keep myself fit for it, later that year I took on a multi-day walk in the central North Island. On the first morning I flew from Taupō in a little four-seater to the airstrip at Boyd Lodge in the headwaters of the Ngaruroro River. I know some hardcore trampers will say that flying in is cheating, but, man, that flight was a buzz.

I've always found the Kaweka and Kaimanawa forest parks fascinating country. The latter in particular is such a complex system of valleys and ridges, with plenty of steep bits, deep rivers to cross and a wonderful sense of remoteness. I left a food drop hanging under the lodge, then set out on a big circuit of the Kaweka Ranges, exploring places I'd never been, poking my nose into old hunters' huts, sidling along tussocky tops. I looped back to Boyd Lodge, then did a short circuit of the Kaimanawas, using mostly unformed backcountry tracks.

It was terrific to be tramping again, but the flights are what stick in the memory. After flying back to Taupō from the Boyd airstrip, I got talking to the charter company's owner, and he invited me for a spin in his little homebuilt aircraft. It was great fun, skimming mountaintops and steep bush slopes, with a few acrobatics thrown in. Eventually, we banked in the direction of Kaimanawa and the Kawekas so I could see from the air all the places I'd just walked through.

Back in Golden Bay, Janet was doing much better. Someone had recommended gardening as a kind of therapy, and she'd thrown herself into it. She had plenty of support around her, and I felt confident she'd be okay if I headed south for a while.

Soon an opportunity presented itself: a two-week conservation trip tidying up hunters' campsites on the remote south-west coast of Stewart Island. When I'd finished, I thought, 'Well, I'm here, and Tekapo's not far away.' I was fit and healthy and keen to spend more time in the backcountry. It felt like the right time to finish my big walk home.

One of the three other guys on the trip was driving up to Queenstown so I tagged along, then hitched to Tekapo. I went to exactly the same café where I'd finished my first leg. Someone there recognised me: 'Aren't you the guy who walked here from Puysegur Point?' 'Yep, and now I'm back to finish the trip.'

I strolled down to the shore for my ritual plunge in the waters, then walked out of town past the Church of the Good Shepherd and the nearby statue of Mackenzie's dog, both of which were swarming with tourists. They all wanted me to pose for photos standing beside the church – the 'Wildman of Tekapo' caught on film, still dripping wet after emerging from the lake.

I made my excuses and walked on around Tekapo's eastern shoreline, searching for the entrance to the Richmond Trail, which follows an old glacial terrace in the foothills above the lake. As I wandered west, I looked up a side creek and saw a pile of metal glinting in the sun. It was the wreck of what looked to be an old Bell 47 helicopter. I've never been able to find out anything about it – there'd clearly been a fire upon impact, so I couldn't even locate the manufacturer's plate to look for a registration number – but I've often wondered about that crash and who was involved.

From the Richmond Trail I climbed up to the Round Hill skifield. My God, skifields are ugly places when the snow has melted and all their workings are exposed. There was detritus lying around, oil, diesel. It was spooky, too – all those shuttered buildings and not a soul to be seen. I felt like I was sneaking around an abandoned village.

The day was hot, dry and dusty, and as I followed the skifield towline up towards 2250-metre-high Mt Musgrave I could feel I'd developed a couple of blisters in my boots, my first blisters for a very long time – decades, even! I put it down to all that dryness in the air following a couple of stream crossings.

No blister was going to distract me from the spectacular views, however. I was high in the foothills of the Two Thumb Range, which runs roughly north to south between Lake Tekapo and one of Canterbury's celebrated braided rivers, the Rangitātā. Since tenure review, a great swathe of it has become part of the DOC estate in the form of the Te Kahui Kaupeka Conservation Park, through which runs a popular section of the Te Araroa Trail. It's charismatic country – big sky, broad glaciated valleys and remarkable mountains, with very little forest apart from the odd tussocky basin with an island of beech trees.

It's also a land of stories, with a history that has snagged me since boyhood. I've mentioned the study of South Island backcountry farming I got into at high school, all those fabled high-country stations. Mesopotamia Station in the Rangitātā Valley where I was heading was probably the most celebrated of them all. Established in 1860 by Samuel Butler (of *Erewhon* fame), who started out with a humble hut beside Forest Creek, it grew to 100,000 acres on the south side of the Rangitātā River, embracing some of the island's most spectacular high country.

More recently I'd got to know the Prouting brothers, whose family has held the Mesopotamia lease since the mid-1940s. Frank Prouting's a keen pilot and every so often he flies into Tākaka from his Marlborough home. He'd taken me for the odd spin, and told me bits and pieces about growing up on the station and some detail about historic musterers' huts in the area, which I was eager to bag.

Near the head of Forest Creek, I saw a big basin and dropped down to a little tarn to camp for the night. It was a lovely spot and I enjoyed one of those calm, bone-dry Mackenzie nights. Next morning as I was packing to leave, a heavy rain arrived out of nowhere. The suddenness of the change was startling.

That day I came upon one of those musterers' huts, but this one was more obscure than most and not marked on any map. I was following the Bush Stream, which flows down through steep country to the Rangitātā, when I caught a glimpse of something man-made among the tussocks. I found a hunched, low-roofed hut, its walls made from sheets of corrugated iron set on their sides and stitched together with old-style steel pickets, with a naturally sloping bank at the back so that if it snowed it would be nicely protected.

The door was another piece of iron propped against the entrance. You had to enter crouching, but once inside you were in complete shelter. There was a stool and what looked like old closed-cell sleeping mats. A former musterer later told me that this kind of hut was pretty common in the local backcountry and often used by deer hunters. The simplicity and effectiveness of the structure impressed me, and it was so cosy. If it wasn't the middle of the day, I would have happily slept there, but I had more ground to cover.

Instead, I spent that night at Stone Hut, a basic eight-bunk musterers' hut that's had its share of tough times, including being partly destroyed by an avalanche in 1967. As a result of the repairs, it's more corrugated iron than stone these days, but I found it comfortable enough and in surprisingly good nick.

*

A quick aside about the musterers' huts I stayed at in the high country. Some are now regarded as being of genuine historic interest, and DOC has done a good job of looking after them. But while they're full of character, they're entirely bereft of insulation. Think of a shelter of tin walls, with a tin roof and concrete or dirt floors, in the depths of a Canterbury winter. You have to feel for those poor musterers.

On the insides and outsides of some of these huts, you can still see beautiful looping handwriting where these old-time farm workers wrote their names and the odd piece of news or casual observation. They used lead pencils so the writing has been well preserved, even on the external walls, despite all the extreme weather thrown their way over decades. You read things like 'Winter muster, 1924 – damned cold!', or 'Just back from town and read about the Hyde train disaster'. It made me think about how today we call any writing on walls 'nasty graffiti'. Will that be treasured as history one day, too?

*

The next morning I backtracked a little, then crossed over Bullock Bow Saddle on the Sinclair Range. Near the saddle I met an older couple leading three horses, including a packhorse. They were visiting from the North Island, but they had a deep connection with Mesopotamia Station – they'd met there 40 years earlier. Now they were retracing their old steps, a kind of pilgrimage back to the place where it started for them, with a plan to arrive at Mesopotamia later that day.

It was a wonderful encounter – the first of many that I'd enjoy on this leg of my big walk home, including a couple of chance meetings with people I'd known for years. It also brought to mind a story Frank Prouting had told me about meeting his wife near Royal Hut, which I'd passed the previous day. At the time of their meeting, there was a rough airstrip up that way. Frank had flown in, and from the air he'd spied a figure with a couple of horses below. After he landed, he crossed the river to say 'gidday', and so met his wife. Those stories, the personal ones, deepened my appreciation of the country I was walking through.

Having said that, I do have a habit of being a bit leery whenever I meet people en masse in the backcountry. A few days later, for instance, when I got to the Rangitātā River, I came upon a flash campsite with two big-wheeled 4WDs parked alongside. My first thought was, 'I've just tramped all this way – what are these people doing here?' But it turned out quite differently than I'd anticipated. It was two elderly couples from Christchurch who'd brought their grandchildren to camp in one of their favourite spots, all having a lovely time. They invited me to join them for a cuppa. I thought, 'Gosh, I'm a judgemental, self-righteous bastard! How can I have thought they shouldn't be here?'

While we were yarning, a fisherman popped up from the river bank, and made a beeline to join us, almost immediately followed by the appearance of a clapped-out Suzuki full of yahoo rabbit shooters armed with .22s. We made an unlikely party, but it was all friendly banter.

One of the shooters started talking about his love of the area. 'Yeah,' he said, 'I really enjoy the peace and ...' He paused, fired off a shot at a rabbit 200 metres away. It echoed among the mountains. 'Yeah the peace and quiet, that's what I enjoy.'

The fisherman was Canadian, and of a philosophical bent. While we all sat around with our cups of tea, he spoke. 'You know, we're all here for the same reason – to enjoy the mountains,' he said. 'But because we're human beings we have to bring our props to justify it. Paul needs a pack; I need a fishing rod; you guys need your rifles. But we're all here for the same thing.' He was spot on, too.

Instead of heading downriver to the Mesopotamia homestead, I went up the valley to a side creek called Black Birch Creek. I wanted to check out Dog Kennel Hut, which turned out to be a very basic tin bivvy on the bush edge, with a fireplace outside. On the way I found another hut, Ayres Hut, which wasn't on any map and has since been removed. It was one of several I stumbled across that were 'off the books', but no doubt provided useful shelter to a few people over the years.

Crossing the Rangitātā was potentially going to be tricky. It's one of those rivers where the Te Araroa Trail stops, then restarts on the opposite side of the river valley – a way of saying to walkers 'It's up to you what you do here'. In some cases, locals near those rivers are now offering, for a fee, to transport people down to the nearest bridge, then back to the trail. I decided I'd walk further up the valley and cross it in sections, and apart from one section where it was waist-deep, I had no real dramas.

Between the Rangitātā and Rakaia rivers is the 60,000-hectare Hakatere Conservation Park. Centred on the Ashburton Lakes district, it has some of the country's finest wetlands, clear streams and tarns, and gorgeous bodies of water set among mountains. It had only recently been created when I went through, picking my way up Potts River to make camp among the tussock and matagouri. Next morning I carried on over the tops to subalpine Mystery Lake. All these evocative titles: Mystery Lake; Wild Man Brothers Range; Black Birch Creek; Mesopotamia – who says New Zealanders can't coin inventive place names!

I sidled into Boundary Creek, then dropped steeply back into the Potts River for a rest day at Potts Hut, which at the time was in transition from being a musterers' hut to a restored historic shelter for public use. Again, the walls were inscribed with writing, including one account that made my hair stand on end. It described how a bunch of men had experienced trouble moving sheep down the valley during a winter muster and been caught out by nightfall. With the temperature plummeting, they set fire to the tussocks, which they said not only gave them warmth and light but also moved the sheep in the right direction. It's written in a self-congratulatory way, like they'd solved this terrible dilemma that could have led to them all dying of exposure up there. No conservation ethic, of course!

From there I climbed over a few passes and up side creeks to the head of the Ashburton River for a night at Top Hut, then down the valley to Wild Man Hut on Mt Arrowsmith Station at the foot of the Wild Man Range, which becomes Wild Man Brothers Range. The toilet there was labelled the 'Wild Man Thunderbox', which made me laugh.

Eventually, I got all the way through to the Rakaia River Valley. This was familiar territory: in 1988, I'd come through the Rakaia around the halfway mark of my 28-day solo traverse from the West Coast. On that trip I'd briefly stopped at Manuka Point Station, near the confluence of the Rakaia and Mathias rivers, and got talking to a young lad at the homestead. On this return visit, I found he was managing the place. When I mentioned our first meeting he said, 'I think I remember that. You were doing a long solo trip, right?'

There'd been big changes at Manuka Point in the intervening 20 years as the owners had shifted focus from farming to high-end trophy hunting for international clients, taking advantage of the property's populations of red stag, fallow deer, tahr and chamois, and its spectacular setting. Coincidentally, that very day they were about to open a beautiful new hunting lodge. I was invited to stick around for the ceremony, and watched as helicopters, jet boats, airplanes and 4WDs converged on the station over the next hours.

One of the choppers was carrying the owner and the manager of nearby Mt Algidus Station. I'd been hoping to get in touch with them for permission to cross the property, and now here they were, landing in my lap. Not only were they happy for me to cross, they offered a bunk in the shearers' quarters if I wanted it.

Mt Algidus is at the end of the Rolleston Range near where the Wilberforce enters the Rakaia. I'd been there twice before. The first visit, in 1974, wasn't in happy circumstances. A multi-day tramping-club trek over the Three Passes route in Arthur's Pass National Park had turned to custard on Whitehorn Pass when a guy went hypothermic and lapsed into unconsciousness. We carried him down to the head of the Wilberforce, rested, then continued down-river to Mt Algidus Station, where the managers put us all up for the night. On my '88 trip I'd also spent a night there.

This time, the lovely South African couple looking after the place were expecting me. They treated me to another memorable night of high-country hospitality – three occasions, three different hosts – and then I retired to the shearers' quarters. Funnily enough, on each visit I slept in the exact same bunk.

Next morning they were heading off to muster sheep and offered to drive me upriver. I couldn't accept – the idea was to walk to Golden Bay under my own steam – but I was happy to take up the offer of a ride for my pack, which I collected from them later in the day after an unencumbered walk up the Wilberforce. From there I crossed the Avoca River and into the Craigieburn Forest Park. My target for the night, Hamilton Hut, was full, as was the Cass Saddle Hut. In the 1970s you might have reasonably expected to have both huts to yourself, but this time I counted 40 people on the track between Hamilton and the saddle. I found a place to camp under some beech trees, and the following day walked out of the wilderness to the Arthur's Pass highway.

By now, my food supplies were starting to look grim, so I decided to hitch to the nearest supermarket – which turned out to be Darfield, 80-odd kilometres back. The Darfield pub looked pretty appealing after so many days in the backcountry, so that night I treated myself to an en suite room and a cooked meal, before taking the bus back to the previous day's finishing point near Cass.

The next evening at Poulter Hut near Minchin Stream I bumped into Peter Jerram, the former Blenheim vet who co-authored a book about veterinary life called *Cock and Bull Stories* a few years ago. I seemed to be always running into Peter or friends of his in the backcountry. I took a rest day and hung out with him and his tramping buddy, and then the next morning we walked together as far as the Minchin Stream Bivvy, where they stayed while I headed over the tops.

I was back at Arthur's Pass, where I'd cut my teeth as a tramper. Familiar surroundings, but I certainly couldn't claim to have walked every trail or stayed at every hut. So rather than plod on towards home, over the next few days I concentrated on side trips into places I hadn't previously explored. From the Poulter Valley I crossed over to Lake Minchin in the shadow of Mt Scarface, then headed along a spur to Minchin Pass. At the Main Divide, I dropped down to Townsend Hut above the Taramakau River, not for the first time marvelling at the suddenness of the transition from open tussockland to lush West Coast rainforest. The hut was right on the bush edge, and that night in my bunk I heard the Christchurch-to-Greymouth freight train rumbling down the valley – an echo of the outside world.

Two days later I made it to Lake Sumner. I'd been there before, but that was 30 years earlier and it almost felt like new country. But then in a sense on every trip it's all new again. You might be following a familiar track, but you're a different person, the weather's different, the conditions won't be the same and neither are your motivations. The country is always shifting – or at least, that's how it is for me.

That was borne out on the next leg, a classic trek following the Kiwi River over the Kiwi Saddle, then a side track up the Hope River to St Jacobs Hut. This was the general neck of the woods where all those years ago I'd laboured in misery up the Tūtaekurī Valley and then had a crack at throwing myself off a cliff, and close to Hope Pass, where I'd managed to cast off some of that gloom. My surroundings brought back memories, but I was an older, hopefully wiser, and certainly happier character, and the landscape held no ghosts for me now. In fact, at St Jacobs Hut my most troubling recollection was of once leaving behind some excellent over-mittens there. I had a deep and long sleep.

Next morning, two guys from the neighbouring station turned up on horseback. They were taking the last sheep off the land before it changed to conservation estate. These guys were the real deal, veteran musterers working the sheep with their dogs and horses. It was the end of an era for that piece of land.

After breakfast, I took a roughly marked route into the Doubtful Range, culminating in a steep half-hour climb to Lake Mann at 1500 metres. People had warned me – 'Lake Mann? Horrible place, terrible weather; you don't want to go up there.' It was the exact opposite, beautifully sunny and serene, with wonderful views.

I descended to the Doubtful River and followed it to a clearing and Doubtful Hut. There I met a fellow whom I just keep bumping into when tramping, Ted Shields. Ted's in his eighties now, and still goes tramping and mountain biking with his son. We caught up over some lunch, and before I left he took a photo of me that's subsequently been used for a few newspaper articles.

*

Devilskin Saddle is the portal between the Doubtful and Nina valleys, and sits high above the Nina River. As I went through I saw that DOC had erected a cute new two-bunk hut above the saddle. It looked cosy and inviting in that raw alpine setting, but I was aiming for shelter further on. I dropped down to the Nina Hut, then followed the Nina Stream for a while before heading up the Lucretia Stream to the Lewis tops and my ultimate goal, the Brass Monkey Hut. It was aptly named: I woke in the night to a bitterly cold wind pounding the walls. It wasn't quite snowing outside, but snow couldn't have been far off. I decided to give myself a break: I'd have a sleep-in and not tramp that day. When you're in a little two-bunk hut beside a picturesque tarn on open tops and the weather is turning grim, you can be forgiven for wanting to put your feet up.

I felt nicely rested by the time I got to the Lewis Pass highway two days later, but my serenity vanished the moment a massive removals truck went barrelling past. On its red side was some white lettering that I swear spelled out the word 'Terminator'. After so many peaceful weeks in the mountains, it was a rude awakening. But then, when you come out of the bush after a decent period of time everything seems louder, faster and more extreme than you remember.

I had a decision to make about my next move. To get from the Lewis Pass to the Kahurangi National Park was necessarily going to take me out of the wilderness, at least for a while. I could have taken the St James Walkway to Nelson Lakes, but then I'd have a big hop west across 'civilised country' to reach the national park. Alternatively, I could bob and weave my way through backcountry as far as Murchison, where I had some friends I was keen to see. Given that the Kahurangi was virtually on their doorstep, it seemed like the better option.

I crossed the highway and walked down the other side of the river and found the track into Lake Daniell. I had a peaceful night beside the lake, then circled the lake and through to the head of Station Creek. There I found a private hut ringed by 4WDs. Turned out this chunk of private land at the creek's head was owned by a 4WD group from Christchurch, mostly families who visit as a group for overnighters. From there, I walked out to the little settlement of Maruia, where I succumbed to temptation in the shape of a $65 motel room with a hot shower and a cooked breakfast.

From Maruia, I continued upriver until I located the entrance to Maruia Saddle Road, part of a network of rough and seldom-used backroads east of the Shenandoah Highway that link to Murchison. A sign said it was closed for vehicles, and I soon saw why. The fords were running deep, and there were great piles of windfall across the road. In fact, it was more track than road in parts, which suited me just fine. I walked on, crossed an ancient 'use-at-your-own-risk' swing bridge to reach the true left side of the Matukituki River, and followed the valley all the way to the highway bridge south of Murchison, where my friends were waiting to collect me.

The following morning, I walked north to Lake Matiri. On previous visits, I'd climbed up to the Thousand Acre Plateau and the Mātiri tops, beautiful and unique plateau country. This time I stuck to the Mātiri Valley, and it proved fascinating in its own right. Looking up I could see scarps scarred raw by rock falls and debris slides, evidence of the forces unleashed by the 1929 Murchison 'quake and the Īnangahua shake four decades later. The 1929 event had erupted great mounds of sand and gravel, creating 'mini volcanoes' on the valley floor. Although I saw none of these, I was aware that Lake Mātiri itself had been created by an earthquake slip. I found it incredibly humbling country, the kind of landscape that just rams home how insignificant we humans are in the face of monumental natural events.

Soon after skirting the edge of tiny Lake Jeanette, I arrived at Hurricane Hut. That night I took my bearings: it was 85.4 kilometres in a straight line to home.

*

Years earlier I'd done a long day walk from the Wangapeka Saddle south along the Mātiri Range to Hurricane Hut; now I was doing the same thing in reverse. There was a heavy mist hanging on the tops, and as I picked my way along the unmarked and in places steep and rocky route, I periodically checked my GPS. I passed a small tarn, dropped down to a scrubby saddle, sidled along a narrow ridgeline, laboured over Nugget Knob, then descended through bush to the Wangapeka Saddle, arriving at Stone Hut just on dark.

There was a big fella sitting on the deck. I greeted him, and in a heavy Ocker accent he replied, 'Gidday, you must be Paul Kilgour.' I was gobsmacked: 'How the hell do you know that?' He informed me that we'd once talked on the phone. 'I rang you from Brisbane once,' he said. 'I'd recognise your voice anywhere.'

It was Tom, a businessman from Brisbane who'd called me perhaps eight years earlier to pick my brains about walking in the Kahurangi National Park. Australians have 'bushwalkers' clubs – they don't use the word 'tramper' – but this guy Tom and his friends have created the 'Brisbane Trampers Club' and every year they fly via Auckland to Nelson, and go tramping for two weeks in the park. They've got a huge soft spot for the Kahurangi, and it's such vast country and such a complex system of valleys and tracks that they can happily keep coming back and enjoying it afresh.

Tom and his mates were on their last night in the park before heading home. When I told them what I was up to they were so impressed they pooled their leftover supplies for me – all very nice grub. I thought, what a hoot: here I am on home turf, and I'm experiencing backcountry hospitality from a bunch of Aussies!

The next day was raining. I retraced my steps to the Wangapeka Saddle and scrambled down into the headwaters of the Taipō and Karamea rivers. I poked my head in at the Trevor Carter Hut, which I hadn't visited before, then headed down the Karamea Valley.

In a bush clearing above the river I found the new Venus Hut. When I say new, I mean that the builders were still in residence applying the finishing touches. I'd bagged it before any other tramper had even set eyes on the thing!

I walked in and the older one of the two builders said, 'Paul Kilgour! How are you, you old bastard? I haven't seen you since 1974.' It was Dave Ogle, a former Forest Service hunter from my Marlborough days. As he'd noted, that meeting was in 1974, at Gosling Hut off the Waihopai Valley. I'd battled through atrocious weather, and found a hunter huddled by the fire. He'd been working out of another hut in the headwaters of a neighbouring stream, and while hunting on the tops had got completely disorientated in mist and ended up in the wrong valley. He had no food with him to speak of, no sleeping bag, and he was drenched and freezing. Between my bag liner and some spare clothes and food, I helped him out, and the next morning showed him a route over the tops.

Decades later, we were meeting again at another hut. Dave and his English offsider were about to start cleaning up the hut in readiness for its official opening. That night they fed me up, and the next morning I helped them sweep the offcuts into a pile to be taken out by heli, then hit the track.

By now I was into deeply familiar country, and the next few days felt a bit like ticking off a list of greatest hits: Karamea Bend, Mt Arthur Tablelands, Balloon Hut, the Cobb Valley. At Myttons Hut, a stone's throw from the Cobb Reservoir, I went to my bunk thinking, 'Golden Bay! I'm home!'

The next day I walked 90 minutes to the base of the Cobb Valley. Janet had rented a little cottage near the DOC staff hut, and she and a couple of friends from the US were planning to drive there to meet me later in the day. It was a frosty morning and I arrived to see smoke coming out of

DOC's chimney. A department worker greeted me: 'Paul, I've been expecting you! I've got the porridge and coffee on.'

I went over to the cottage and had a bit of a clean-up and got my washing done, then around midday Janet and friends arrived. It was fantastic to see her, but the Americans, a mother and daughter who were meeting me for the first time, seemed taken aback. I'd broken a cap off a front tooth, and my beard and hair had seen better days. I must have looked to them like a toothless old mountain man!

I was home, but I wasn't quite *home*. I had a couple more days of walking ahead of me, starting with the Ragged Trail, the one from the Cobb power station where my mate got himself lost. It's called the Ragged Trail because in the 1970s it was marked with rags. One of the power station workers who was a keen hunter used to raid the rag bin and shred thin strips to mark his way into the mountains. They'd deteriorated over the years, all the wool, cotton, denim and synthetics, but the good old tartan had hung in there: slightly faded but still highly visible markers. So off I went, following a marked route that I'd taken several times before. Home and a good long rest were just around the corner.

Eventually the Ragged Trail brings you to a ridge, which unfortunately in places isn't well defined and tends to zig-zag. I was nearing that spot where my friend had got himself confused when I suddenly thought, 'Hang on, where am I?' I'd done exactly the same thing as my mate, stepped off the ridge in one direction, convinced that I'd gone the other. I couldn't believe it. After walking nearly the length of the South Island without incident, I was lost in my own backyard.

I'd given Janet all my gear, but I still had my GPS and my phone. I thought about phoning her to get a grid reference, but even as I was contemplating that embarrassing conversation, I came across the track. I followed it for a while and found footsteps. Recent ones, same size as mine and going in the opposite direction. It took a long moment for my brain to accept that I'd gone in a circle. I can see how with pilots, their mind sometimes wants to override what their instruments are telling them; I had that same reaction. But I took a deep breath, calmed myself and figured it out.

Eventually, I found my way through to the Kill Devil track, a historic mining pack track that climbs from the Tākaka Valley into the Lockett Range. Along the trail you pass several historic gold miners' bivvies, but I stayed that night at Riordans Hut, which was built in the 1920s by two farming brothers as a musterers' hut and has been nicely restored. The next morning I took a secret side trail to a property where some good friends of mine, the Stones, lived with their five children.

After a cuppa to celebrate my return to Golden Bay, there was a long day walk down the Tākaka River – always a good option for getting across farmland and through civilised country – as far as Paynes Ford. My plan was to cross at the mouth of the Tākaka, then walk around the Rangihaeata headland to home, but I had some time to kill before low tide. So, I walked to my favourite café in town, where the owner shouted me lunch as a 'good on you' gesture for completing the trip.

When I got to the river mouth, it was approaching low tide. I still had to cross in chest-high water, but I was so close now I didn't care about being wet. I walked, squelching, around the coast, up to the house, in the front door and said, 'I'm home!'

I'd walked 36 days from Tekapo. Adding the first leg from Puysegur Point, I'd walked 84 days, plus 15 rest days. As the crow flies, it was a distance of 774 kilometres, but I'd walked 1546. I'd lost a bunch of weight, my ribcage was almost skeletal, but I still seemed to have energy to burn. I was home, but part of me wanted to keep walking.

After I stopped, the world suddenly seemed so noisy. Even on our quiet street, where we see few cars, when one drove past I'd find it almost overwhelming: 'Whoa, too much!' As for the radio or the TV, it was an assault. One day Janet found a whistle in with some old tramping gear, and blew it. 'Please, no!' The smell of fumes affected me, too. When an aircraft flew overhead, the whiff of fuel got me. It took me at least a couple of weeks to settle back into normal life.

I reflected on the two legs of my walk home and was struck by the contrast. In the south, it had been a journey of high alps and big, open country, the kind that expands the mind. Despite walking in the height of summer, there'd been snow in my field of vision most of the time. From Albert Burn Saddle, I'd looked across at Aspiring's mantle of perma-snow, and north to Aoraki/Mt Cook's white flanks.

From Arthur's Pass north the change of landscape and mood was dramatic. There'd been forays through beech forest and a side trip into the nurturing West Coast bush. The waterways had transformed, too, from those mighty southern rivers that flow east of the Main Divide, a tangle of braids across vast gravel plains, to the likes of the Karamea, rolling through beech and mixed podocarp forest.

I felt a quiet sense of pride – not so much for the distance covered, but the way I'd handled it. I'd taken one step at a time, and every step had been enjoyed, every step was meaningful. Really, that's the only way we can approach life. Otherwise it becomes a confused blur, and negativity can creep in.

Royal Hut, Bush Stream, Two Thumbs Range, 2009.

Chapter 27

I've been tramping for half a century. That's more than long enough to have become aware of the downward spiral of our native species. In the 1970s, we took for granted hearing kiwi calling from the bush at night. Even then the dawn chorus was still a thing to behold. But it has been nearly snuffed out in places, and the loss crept up on us. During the 1980s in the Abel Tasman, the babbling of people grew in inverse proportion to the birdsong; we complained about the growing crowds, but we were less tuned in to the rapid decline of the birds.

After decades of walking and enjoying the backcountry, I feel I need to give back. That's why I'm involved in the Permolat group – I want to help save some of these huts that have served me so well. It's also part of the reason why I've dedicated myself to conservation projects, particularly predator control. The other thing that motivates me is a sense of not wanting to surrender to feelings of depression and helplessness. Environmental degradation has always got to me, so I'm keen to grab any opportunity to get out of the house and help.

I started about ten years ago with a few traps around our place at Rangihaeata, which at its lowest edge touches the Onahau Estuary, home to nationally threatened banded rails, fern birds, marsh crakes and the odd bittern. The local council announced a permanent trap-loan programme, and I put my hand up for eight traps. Our neighbours got involved, too, and the scheme grew. At the same time, I started trapping on a ten-acre property just up the road, where I'm caretaker.

Today, I can sit on a nearby hill and see a patchwork of protected bush areas. And every time that I walk up the coastline to Collingwood – it takes about five hours if I time it right for the low tide at Parapara Estuary – I come across more of the purple tags that indicate a predator trap. I reckon there must be an almost complete network now that extends from the Aorere River Valley along the coast to the Abel Tasman National Park – and it's all the work of volunteers. I find it inspiring, and I often say to friends who are anti-1080, 'Well, what's stopping you setting up your own trapping programme?'

More recently, I've been volunteering on a carbon-sink initiative in East Tākaka called Project Rameka. It was started by mountain-bike pioneer Jonathan Kennett and his partner Bronwen Wall in 2008 when they bought a 50-hectare block of marginal farmland and pine plantation in the Rameka Valley to replant in natives. Subsequently it has been expanded by another 45 hectares. I find it especially appealing because it incorporates a historic walking trail, the 1850s Rameka Track, which links Golden Bay to Canaan Downs on Tākaka Hill.

I'm also heavily involved, with two other people, in the Project Rameka trapping programme. We've got 120 traps so far, targeting mostly rats and stoats. Recently Janet and I went to a music festival at Canaan Downs – you're never too old! – and the next morning I walked down the Rameka Track to check the traps, and ended up staying overnight. I love camping up there, particularly when it's raining. There's something about being sheltered when it's teeming down and you can be sure no one will be coming. It's an escape from the world – except at Rameka I can retreat while also doing something positive for the land.

As a community, we've established mountain-bike and walking tracks, and every year we plant another 1000 trees or so with Motupipi primary school. We've put in a variety of broadleaf, rimu and kahikatea, and heaps of flax and toetoe. It's all grown by Titoki Nursery near Brightwater, who have permits to collect seed from the edge of the national park just a couple of kilometres from where we're planting. That's important, to get seed sources as close to the project as possible.

Over the years I've done a bit of volunteering for DOC on its endangered species work, signing on for several of what the department calls 'volunteer holidays'. What do I bring? For a start, I'm someone who's able to reach remote backcountry places – with species monitoring work that's invaluable because the birds involved are often in far-flung spots. As for trapping work, I also have an ability to think like a possum or whatever other animal is being trapped, a sense of how they travel through the bush. Over years of tramping you develop those tracking skills.

Once I did a stint of track and hut maintenance for DOC in the Hollyford and Pyke valleys. I remember in the Pyke finding the cableway across the river to the Olivine Hut had rusted in place. We went into the hut hoping for some cooking oil, but instead found rancid margarine. God, it smelled awful, but it did the trick.

Another volunteer trip involved a two-week clean-up of beaches on the western side of Stewart Island. Given the remoteness of the location, it was shocking how much rubbish we found. According to the helicopter pilot, over that fortnight the combined weight of all the sacks we filled was 25 tonnes. I went back a few years later and those same beaches were still colourful with bits of plastic.

In 2003, I was part of a four-person DOC team doing beach clean-ups and hut maintenance at Doubtful Sound. The huts were an eye-opener – and not in a good way. Because they can be accessed by boat, people tend to bring in all sorts of junk, and some left a hell of a mess behind. Still, it was an incredible trip. Using the DOC boat, we went places the tourist cruises never go, and I got to check out some short walks and bag new huts, including a hunters' bivvy on Bauza Island in the outer sound, and Gut Hut on Secretary Island.

I was assigned to check predator traps on the islands. I'd get dropped off – on more rugged islands that generally involved jumping from the front of the boat when the skipper gave the order – then follow the trap lines from one end to the other. Some of the islands were tiny and I'd be finished in ten minutes; one took me three hours. When I was done, I'd radio to be picked up.

That trapping work in Doubtful Sound underscored for me just what we're up against with pest control. You'd see stoat and rat tracks heading into the water, aimed at some offshore island where penguins nested. I'd haul rats out of traps set on islands two or three kilometres from shore – they swim that far! On the mainland, some of the traps were set in places so steep that you could only access them using the boat. Once I climbed onto an almost horizontal rātā tree, then along a branch to a rocky ledge where there was a trap – and found a bloody rat in it. It felt good to be doing something to help, but it was scary to think of these predators out there hunting for bird nesting sites. They're relentless.

*

One of my favourite conservation trips was Codfish Island/ Whenua Hou, the predator-free sanctuary west of Stewart Island that is the focus of kākāpō recovery work. It was a supplement-feeding project, aimed at maintaining the female kākāpō population in healthy condition prior to nesting. With no feeding intervention, these birds will climb up to the top of rimu trees to gorge on the flowers, and sometimes get so stuffed they plummet to the ground. Given the rarity of kākāpō, unsurprisingly that's behaviour DOC wants to discourage.

The kākāpō all had names. One that stood out was Sinbad. You'd be down at the feeding station and suddenly a figure would leap onto you from a bush – Sinbad. Kākāpō have strong claws, and once they latch on it's hard to get them off. They say each of these parrots is worth a million dollars – I'm not sure how you put a value like that on a kākāpō, but that's what I've heard – so when they won't let go you face quite a dilemma. I was instructed to grab the bird by the legs and hold him upside down to disorient him (shades of my farm upbringing, where we used to do exactly the same thing to chickens before we lopped their heads off). Once Sinbad was scrambled, you popped him on a branch and ran like mad.

Then there was Sirocco, the kākāpō who became notorious for his attempts to mate with a BBC reporter's head. Sirocco constantly wandered around the base hut. I found it sad that he'd become so used to human contact. We'd have barbecues at night and sometimes he'd sit on my lap and ever so gently preen my whiskers.

I went to Codfish Island to help, but I got at least as much from the experience as the birds did. It was magical, particularly those evenings when the kākāpō were booming. It's a sound that totally resonates through your body, more powerful than any rock festival. To hear four male parrots calling out in the night forest was a performance I won't forget.

Closer to home, I've helped with trap monitoring as part of DOC's blue duck/whio recovery programme in the south branch of the Wangapeka. We established ourselves at Boyd Hut, an old tramping hut that DOC helicoptered in from Mt Owen to be a base for its whio work. It was good fun exploring some of those remote backcountry streams, zig-zagging over ridges, checking traps, and I was impressed by what they'd achieved. There's a huge network of trap lines running through that south branch area, and I saw plenty of whio in the streams.

Promising signs, too, in the Abel Tasman and the Heaphy. I've noticed an amazing increase in birdsong on both tracks, and it's starting to spill out to surrounding areas – the halo effect, they call it. One of the kākā released into the bush at Bark Bay in 2019 has established a nesting site just a couple of kilometres from Project Rameka, and I saw five kea in there recently. The old pine trees on the property are rotting and falling over and they're full of huhu and other grubs that kākā and kea love, so I'm hoping they pay us more regular visits.

Lucretia Biv, Lewis Pass.

Chapter 28

As a tramper with many miles under his belt I'm more conscious than most of the ways the backcountry is changing. Sometimes, the shift can be sudden and violent. Recall the caravan-sized boulder that nearly flattened me and my tramping friends above Lake Wilmot, in Fiordland National Park? That rock had once been part of a mountaintop, and then had rested on a ledge above the river for millions of years, until its time to move arrived. After our hearts had stopped racing, we all agreed that it was a humbling thing, to witness an aeons-long geological process culminate so dramatically like that in front of us.

Other transitions I've witnessed have been decades in the making – although in geological time that's still lightning quick. In 1983 when I lived and worked at Mt Cook, I often crossed the terminus of the Tasman Glacier on my way to the Murchison Valley. Less than 40 years later, there's now a great body of glacial water there called Tasman Lake, and if you have the money you can take a boat tour among icebergs. It's the same up the Hooker Valley where in '83 I took my morning runs – more glacial retreat and another large melt lake. As for the Ball Hut Road up the Tasman Valley where I used to drive the tour bus, that's now gone completely, with not even a terrace between the steep mountainside and the edge of the glacier.

I wrote earlier about seeing the scars of historic earthquakes in the Mātiri Valley. I've also explored the Clarence River Valley before and after the Kaikōura 'quake. The changes I saw from my earlier trips up the Clarence were astonishing. I didn't so much feel humbled as awed by what nature had unleashed there.

Weather, too. I do a lot of tramping up the Anatoki River Valley, where you cross a lot of side creeks and they're constantly changing. A gentle stream I previously crossed in a couple of steps will have transformed since my last trip into a torrent pouring through a canyon gouged from the hillside. In some West Coast river valleys I've walked through, you can tell from the age of the trees that the river has flowed its particular course for hundreds and hundreds of years; but then a storm will alter it overnight. Likewise where we live, a king tide collides with a major storm and suddenly five metres of coast has gone.

It's not only the landscape and weather that has altered. During my 50 years on the hoof, there have also been big developments in the way the outdoors is used and enjoyed, and by whom. Again, I think of Aoraki/Mt Cook in 1983. On my days off I would venture into the Hooker Valley, where at the time very few other people went. Sometimes I wouldn't see a soul for the entire day, and the only sounds were pipits, kea and the distant crashing of avalanches. It was a peaceful alpine idyll, and especially lovely when the wild flowers were in bloom. Now it has been discovered by mainstream tourists and it's an entirely different scenario, with hundreds of visitors lining up to cross the swing bridges, while the flash new boardwalks resonate with the thumping of a thousand footsteps.

The upgrading of tracks and huts has brought more people into the backcountry, and getting off the beaten track has become a tougher ask. When I lived at the Tui Community I would regularly walk around what was then called the Coastal Track in the Abel Tasman and be confident of peace and solitude. Now it's a highway.

Is it all bad? That's a tricky one. I feel lucky to have experienced both before and after, but I suspect I've known the best. It is a good thing to share this beautiful country, but I've seen too many instances where we seem to be milking it for all we can without thinking about consequences. Values seem to have been shelved in the name of coining foreign currency.

It's easy to fixate on the negative, and to overstate things, but I believe that something of the traditional backcountry culture has eroded. On that solo tramp into the Rakaia Valley in the 1980s that I mentioned, I met a farm worker who casually told me to head to the station homestead and pretty much help myself – 'leave your mail on the table, we'll post it; use the phone; and while you're at it, help yourself to tea and biscuits'. That trust and hospitality always impressed me, but I wonder if it's still as prevalent now.

When I started walking, trampers were generally pretty down-to-earth people, and because there were so few of us we tended to be pleased to see each other. We'd leave food at huts for whomever came next, and share things when we met. We were birds of a feather. Now it's more of a tourist thing. There are more gear-freaks and more one-upmanship, and outdoor clothing has become a fashion statement. There has been a change in the nature of tramping, too. Because people tend to be so time-poor, more of us are getting a helicopter or fixed wing into one end of a multi-day tramping track and being flown out from the other.

Likewise, sources of information have changed. In the 1970s, you'd walk into a ranger's house somewhere such as St

Arnaud in the Nelson Lakes and their lounge was the information centre. They were such knowledgeable individuals about their patch and could talk in detail about the surrounding tracks, the dangers and pleasures. A ranger's number-one priority was keeping trampers informed and safe, and they would often be out walking the tracks gathering useful intelligence to pass on. Today, you're expected to go online. Visit a regional i-SITE or DOC office and the people working there tend to be excellent at selling wilderness 'product', but not so hot when it comes to useable tramping tidbits. Often, they'll pass you on to someone local. 'You want some information about walking in the Kahurangi National Park? How about I give you Paul Kilgour's number?'

You have to be sceptical about what you find online about tracks and routes, too. A lot of people now post their trip reports, and they're often taken as gospel by people planning a walk into unfamiliar country. But I've found plenty of examples that were unreliable on key details. I still rate the Moir's guidebooks, however, which continue to be written by genuine backcountry people of a similar age and experience to me. The books do have their shortcomings – I've corrected the odd thing, like 'that's not a two-bunk bivvy, it's an eight-bunk musterers' hut' – but they're far more accurate on the important stuff than most.

The other oracle that I suspect won't ever let me down is the local pub. When I'm really struggling to find in-depth information on a piece of backcountry, I'll phone the nearest tavern. Often, the local expert will be nursing a pint in the garden bar.

Other developments I regard more neutrally. The development of tramping gear, for instance. When I started out a watch had one function – telling time! You can now spend a small fortune on various electronic gizmos, super-engineered backpacks, and tents that have been developed to the nth degree to make your trip a pleasurable and safe experience. Most of it I can do without, but something like the Aarn pack has just been a godsend for me, and I'm sure it will extend my tramping life well beyond what I might have other otherwise achieved.

*

I imagine that raises a question: How long can he go on? I'm 70 now, an age at which a lot of backcountry stalwarts have long since hung up their boots. Until recently, however, I had no intention of slowing down – it's been forced on me by injuries.

A few years ago I had what I thought at the time was a pretty innocuous slip on day 13 of a three-week walk in the Clarence River Valley that damaged both of my Achilles. Perhaps unwisely, I chose not to activate my locator beacon. I figured, 'Look this isn't life-threatening and you're a week from panic day.' Plus, I had plenty of food and supplies stashed ready to collect in the next hut, which was only four hours' walk away. I didn't realise that it was going to take me 19 hours over two days to limp there.

The Clarence is dry country, all matagouri, tussock and brambles. I was following a 4WD track, but my progress was snail-like. It was hot and I was terribly thirsty, but a plague of Canada geese had fouled the waterways. Finally, I found a little spring under some wild roses and drank deep. It was obvious by now I wasn't going to get anywhere near the hut, so I started looking for a spot to pitch my tent where I wasn't going to get trampled by cattle. As it happened, something did walk over me in the night – a goose! It gave me a hell of a fright. The pain was no better when I woke, and it was another long, limping day to reach the hut, and another three days before some hunters turned up and drove me out to Kaikōura.

The injury was subsequently misdiagnosed. A typical scenario: a rural doctor, totally overworked, mistook it for a stress fracture of a fibula in one leg. I'd just turned 65 and learned that I was now officially an 'old person', for whom stress fractures are just another occupational hazard of the 'golden years'. For 18 months I struggled with that misdiagnosis, while the injury got worse and worse. I tried a few gentle walks, but was in agony. It was incredibly frustrating being unable to get back into the hills. Finally, I consulted a physio. Within ten minutes, she'd diagnosed two damaged Achilles, one torn and one herniated.

The injury troubling me now is my knee, which I damaged just before the first 2020 lockdown. I was hobbling around the annual WOMAD festival in New Plymouth, and the medical people there told me I'd torn a knee ligament.

I had some physio and it seemed to be improving, but then early last summer I aggravated it while doing a five-day trip with a friend, a classic traverse ticking off the Anatoki River, Adelaide Tarn, Boulder Lake and through to the end of Aorere Valley near Bainham. The knee got really sore in the last couple of hours, and walking across a farm paddock to our waiting vehicle I gave it a mild twist. Not long ago, the knee gave way again. I was in town and I fell on the ground in front of some people. They all gathered around. I got quite emotional because this thing with my knee has been going on too long. It's destroyed a summer of tramping.

*

It would be easy to get down, and I have had my blue moments, but from our house I can look out and see Parapara Peak and the Anatoki Mountains and think, 'Yep, that's pretty good motivation!' And Janet encourages me to keep walking.

Recently we were down in Central Otago and did some short walks to places I've never been before, the likes of the Rob Roy Track near Wānaka – places that are usually so crowded with tour buses that I've never felt the urge to visit. Suddenly all these overpopulated spots are delightful to explore, and I've ticked a few off my list.

Until my knee comes right, however, I'm going to have to stick to these shorter walks and modify my tramping style. I've never considered myself a particularly fast tramper, more of the steady-as-she-goes type, capable of plodding along happily for great distances, but I'm now consciously walking a bit slower. I'm also using walking poles. I started with the classic Leki poles, but they gave me sore wrists, so I've switched to an English product called the Pacerpole that has ergonomically designed right and left hand grips. With less stress on your wrists you can put a heap more power into your arms, and I've found my upper arm muscles are becoming more developed – a welcome bonus! Throw in my trusty Aarn pack and it's a potent combination, with the pack keeping my centre of gravity vertical and the arm-pumping putting a nice extension on my spine.

*

I have a laundry list of backcountry trips I want to do. A while ago, I started jotting them down in a school notebook. Whenever I hear about a new route guide or read a description of an intriguing-sounding hut or track system or someone's account of a trip to a place I haven't visited, I add it to the mix. I've filled three notebooks and I'm now working on the fourth. So there is never an end, even after all these decades of tramping.

In particular, I have my eye on two 'bucket list' walks as soon as my knee is up for it. One is a trip from Karamea to Golden Bay, my familiar stomping ground, but I'd be taking what would be a new route for me, trekking up the Lower Karamea River, then branching off up the Ugly River, through the Tasman Mountains and Domett Range to Lake Aorere, then down the Roaring Lion to the Cobb Valley. The other is a three-week coast-to-coast traverse, starting at Ross on the West Coast, and working my way through the various mountains in the Hokitika Conservancy and Arthur's Pass National Park. The halfway point would be Ōtira, and from there I'd head into the headwaters of the Poulter River and the tributaries of the Puketeraki Range, through the Lees Valley to the Mt Thomas Conservation Area and down the Ashley River, which flows to the coast just north-east of Rangiora. That one would incorporate a lot of new country, as well as unfamiliar track systems and a bunch of huts that the Permolat people have restored that I'd love to bag. I'd finish by walking down the coast to Kaiapoi.

How about a second epic traverse, in the style of my big walk home? Maybe. It's a hard act to follow, and I'm a dozen years older and more weather-worn, but you never know. Whatever form my next wanderings take, if I'm in the bush or beside a backcountry river I'll be happy. One step at a time is really good walking.

Acknowledgments

I acknowledge all those who have inspired, supported and encouraged me along life's journeys. There have been so many wonderful folk, many whose names have been lost in the mists of time.

Family members have helped me to become myself.

Grandfather Silas shared his childhood adventures of growing up near the Snowy Mountains in New South Wales, Australia.

Nana Ivy shared her childhood adventures from Jersey Island in the English Channel Islands.

My father, Bob, encouraged me to keep up, as he strode over the steep hills on our farm at Waimauku. He gave me news clippings and photos of trampers exploring the beautiful high country of the South Island.

My mother, Dorna, fed me well with her delicious home cooking.

My brothers, Barry and Ross, shared some adventurous tramping journeys from the coast to the mountains. They have also been happy to provide drop-offs and pick-ups at remote road ends.

My daughter, Sequoia, shared her deep knowledge of the Australian bush and its wonderful wildlife near her home in Queensland, Australia. We also shared walks and overnight tramping trips in New Zealand and Australia.

Her five boys, my grandsons, Raven, Sky, Julian, Benedict and Simmy, help me to feel young again as I experience the world through their escapades.

My nephew Cameron shares with me his deep botanical knowledge, especially of forest floor and alpine plant life.

Some delightful adventures and 'Bot Fests' have been had together.

My partner, Janet, forever encourages me to get out there and enjoy the hills. She has accompanied me and supported me on tramping trips and intrepid journeys to Australia, the Cook Islands, Fiji, Vanuatu, Rotuma Island, Tonga, Hawaii, mainland USA, Alaska and Canada.

The Marlborough Tramping Club and the Golden Bay Alpine and Tramping Club have provided many character-developing and inspirational trips.

And last but by no means least, to all those lovely people who have supported and encouraged me in so many ways. This includes tramping mates and companions. There are so many of them and too many to list here. Thanks to each and everyone of you. Our cherished memories will last forever.

Journey well.